UNCOILING THE SERPENT:

Kundalini & the Dynamics of Spiritual Maturity

by

John Lawrence Maerz

Published in the United States by

Emotional Troubleshooter

ISBN 978-1-7372493-8-2

Other Books by JOHN LAWRENCE MAERZ

TAROT: *The Astrological Layout*

CYCLES: *The Application of Energy Within the Natural Cycle*

A MILE IN YOUR SHOES: *The Road to Self-Actualization Through Compassion*

IS ANYONE THERE? *Reaching Behind the Veil in Mediumship*

ENERGIZING SELF-TRUST: *7 Steps for Reclaiming Your Power*

OUT OF THE BOX: *7 Elements for Raising a Self-Directing Child*

SIGNS & PORTENTS: *Reader's Guide for Combining Psychic Tools*

PLOYS FOR DOMINANCE: *A Guide for Recognizing & Disarming Manipulation*

NUMEROLOGY: *Life's Mirror of Vibration*

ASTROLOGY 4 PURPOSE, POWER & PERSPECTIVE: *A Primer for the Seven Rays & the Work of Alice Bailey*

IN THE WORLD BUT NOT OF IT: *Heaven, Hell & the Many Faces of Enlightenment & Ascension*

UNWINDING THE KARMIC WHEEL: *The Journey from Survival to Compassion*

CORE VALUES: *Recognizing & Surviving the Global Assault on Our Personal Autonomy*

~ Experience is the Greatest Teacher ~

~ Hear-say is the Greatest Deceiver ~

TABEL OF CONTENTS

INTRODUCTION

The study and practice of spirituality has gone through tremendous changes over the last hundred years. Although the path of ascension remains the same, our assumption on how to pursue it has become clouded in methods, gimmicks and shortcuts which assume that there is an easier way to spiritual maturity than the tried-and-true ancient paths. Nothing could be further from the truth. It still requires strength, diligence and sensitivity.

It is delusional to believe that escaping from physical reality will promote the embodiment of spirituality. Yet, many who profess toward being spiritual tout withdrawal from participating in the physical world as *the* productive path toward becoming more spiritually mature. In and of itself, withdrawing from physical reality and claiming to be more spiritual because of it is simply self-deceptive. It negates self-awareness and the integration of our emotional and intuitive capacities within the tangible world. However, when we do withdraw from physical reality in order to develop a meditative state, it *can* be productive toward developing spiritual maturity if it is with the intention of making the centered and relaxed headspace applicable toward its integration with physical reality. Few people can even conceive of this, let alone understand it.

Historically, respect has often been a byproduct of attaining a better alignment with our inner spirit. The main benefit is augmented self-respect and a feeling of accomplishment. A supplemental benefit might be the respect that we harvest from those who observe and admire the strength and effectiveness of our efforts although it is not our primary objective. Unfortunately, there are also those who will feel jealousy over our personal success and, childishly, do what they can to diminish the merit of our accomplishments. What is necessary for us to understand is that we must *not* respond to their discouragement. It is not spiritually productive to argue with those who are filled with jealousy and come at us from a position of low *self-worth*.

The premise of spiritual development has been a context from which many people of moderate to low *self-worth* have used to acquire a social standing and a status of augmented personal worth in the eyes of others. In this light, and to them, the acquisition of such a status is generally more important than the actual growth that might occur if the path is pursued with the intention of intellectually and emotionally maturing in the interest of becoming more self-aware and accountable for their earthly existence.

Our spiritual development is one of constant vigilance and constant striving to maintain our spirit's cleanliness. This means avoiding falling into behaviors characteristic of the seven vices and manifesting behaviors characteristic of the seven virtues. There is no "owing." There is no obligation to give back to society. There is only the opportunity for us to purify our actions and objectives simply to fulfill our conscious reunion with the universe and acquiesce to its natural laws in spite of our human frailties.

Part 1

ENERGY BASICS

RAISING ENERGY

Is That What Really Happens?

Raising energy has been a buzz phrase used through the metaphysical community and through our secular culture for many years. For the secular culture it's simply "getting psyched" or getting into the "headspace" to do some activity or task. For the metaphysical community it relates to "building a charge" so we might move smoothly through something we might not ordinarily do in our daily tangible activities. For both, they may employ different perspectives to do so but the end result will essentially be the same. We become powered up for performing. But what is actually happening?

Do we really *raise energy,* or do we simply put ourselves in a "headspace" for a special activity? The truth is, we really don't *raise energy* because, whether we realize it or not, it is already there and at our disposal, but we simply don't have access to it at the moment. Why? Let's first look at a "headspace" activity to get a better understanding of what we're dealing with.

Unless you're a dedicated workaholic, we all have hobbies and activities that we enjoy spending our time doing. These activities don't necessarily "contribute" anything to our support or life maintenance and allow us to enjoy some "me" time. They are primarily a pastime that allows us to disconnect from our daily stresses. The dedicated workaholic would view this as wasting our time or avoiding our responsibilities. But if we allow ourselves to become immersed in the activity, time stops, our stresses lessen, and we emerge from the activity refreshed and energized. Sometimes we become so immersed that hours can seem like minutes. We've all had activities that we become involved in and find that much more time has passed than we had thought. This is one of the ways that we feel that we have *raised energy*. But did we actually *raise* energy? No. We simply distracted ourselves from unpleasant and challenging issues by removing from our consciousness most of the undesirable feelings and activities that were *drawing on* and *occupying* our energy. Also, notice that I did not say *depleting* our energy. Our energy is still with us but otherwise occupied.

Since energy can neither be created nor destroyed, it is always with us. In this light, it *cannot* be raised. It can only be freed from whatever is *occupying* it. And whatever is *occupying* it is there because our intention and consciousness has put it there. This says *everything* about our intention and our focus.

So, to recap, we don't *raise energy*, we simply redirect it.

ENERGY FOLLOWS THOUGHT

Let's look a little deeper into the dynamics of energy. *Energy follows thought*. It is a commodity. *It is mindless.* It goes exactly where we put it. If we focus on distressing issues, it will be invested in what we are challenged by. If we focus on enjoyable things, we will move smoothly through the activity and it will be freed from any of the prevailing conscious obsessions or compulsions we normally direct it toward. The hardest part of this that faces our consciousness is for us to first, recognize *what* our mind is obsessed with and, second, recognize that *all we have to do is change the channel*. But that's a much harder nut to crack than we think.

Primarily, the most virulent coercion for keeping our energy focused on "responsible" tasks is the belief that our responsibility to the world and what it expects of us is much more important than our own happiness and well-being. Secondly, we believe that our abdication of that responsibility immeasurably damages our public image. Hence, we almost never give ourselves permission to enjoy ourselves. And if we do, we feel that we must hide it from others or make excuses for it for fear of being seen as being frivolous or irresponsible. This ultimately crashes our sense of *self-worth*.

When this kind of "responsibility" occupies the focus of our energy, there is not much left to do anything else. It blocks our use of energy for anything playful or enjoyable. We've made changing the channel of where we apply our energy virtually impossible by labeling it as impermissible. So, on top of this, when we say we need to *raise energy*, we're only fooling ourselves that we can willfully conjure up anything more. Truthfully, our only option is to diminish the use of it in the obsessions and compulsions we've focused it on.

So, essentially, we do not *raise energy*, we simply redirect it. We can make it available by freeing it through changing the channel of where we are applying it, hence, *energy follows thought*. We can do this through focusing our mind and attention on hobbies, meditation and activities that will break our obsessions and compulsions diverting our attention away from the things that cause us stress and aggravation. We also do this when we sleep. This is why catnaps are so recharging. When we sleep, the mind literally let's go of our conscious focus and the body is able to use the *freed energy* to regenerate and revitalize us. We usually wake up fresh and recharged…until we resume the same stress that produced energy hungry activities and thinking.

THE MIND IS ONLY A TOOL

The mind is a wonderful *tool*. We *are not* our minds. We *have* a mind. Renes Descartes said, "I think, therefore, I am." That puts a whole lot of emphasis on our mind being the central point of our being. It's not. We should rather say, "I am, therefore I think." This relegates our minds to simply being a *tool* that is *employed* by "something" else. That something else is our *spirit*, our *soul* and *the Witness*. This part of us is simply an observer and has total access to our energy. When we put our headspace here, the mind is prevented from occupying our energy. Our *spirit* has total energy availability.

So, do you need an energy recharge? Paint, dance, read, meditate, sleep or do any activity that will absorb all of your attention. This changes the channel. It will "unclench" your mind and reduce your tension and you will come back to feeling like you've just *raised your energy.*

DUMPERS, DRAINERS & DRONES

In the metaphysical community it is a commonly held fallacy that others can *drain* our energy. Truthfully, they don't *take* it from us, we actually allow them to free themselves of *their* tension by our acceptance of it through applying *our* attention (energy) to *their* concerns. This consequently binds *our* energy to *their* problems. This is essentially not our being *drained* but their *"dumping"* on us. There is no "exchange" of energy but only a transference of tension producing thoughts. This is how it works.

In the same way that we free our energy from occupation by applying it to something we find pleasure in doing, others feel that freedom by unburdening themselves by "giving us" the burden of what they were mentally obsessed with through our acceptance of it by applying attention to it. It operates much the same way like a confession relieves the pressure of carrying guilt over a deed we've committed that contradicts our values. Both of our energies remain unchanged. The only thing that has changed is where we have each focused it. *They* can release their preoccupation, by *our choosing* to take it on. The key in understanding the dynamic is that we *choose* to accept the tension through our applying *our* attention (energy) to it. *This* binds our energy and makes us feel like we've been drained. Essentially, their "confession" becomes a *dumping* on us.

To accept someone else's tension, we must be susceptible to one of two emotional "hooks." We must be either interested enough in gaining something through the subject presented by the *"dumper"* to participate in a dialogue with them or we must be *guilted into having to participate* in lieu of appearing to be inconsiderate or selfish. In short, we must have a personal motive to participate.

A *drone* operates through the same process but with an added dimension. That dimension is a persistence their *dumping* until we give up defending ourselves and take on their tension. Once we've taken on their stress by giving it our energy and attention (we want to be and appear compassionate), they can move past our resistance and have an open door to easily *dump* the totality of their distress on us. Mind you, it is still we who have chosen to let them do so. The key for us is to recognize who they are, what they are doing and to not allow the *dump* to take place.

ENERGY EMPOWERS MOVEMENT

Energy empowers movement. If there's no energy, there's no movement. When anything moves, it moves in cycles and circles. Days cycle between light and dark. Seasons cyclically repeat themselves. Water goes down the drain in a circular motion. Tornadoes and hurricanes go in circles. Galaxies move and are shaped in spirals. Planets circle around the Sun. Electrons circle atoms. Planets rotate on their axes. If anything moves, it moves in a circular manner. Energy is no different. When energy moves toward or away from us, we add a new dimension. It will move either counterclockwise or clockwise (CCW or CW).

When energy moves toward us, it moves in a counterclockwise direction. When it moves away from us, it moves in a clockwise direction. What needs to be added for us to understand its movement relative to us is our point of perspective. This is where things become sticky and confusing for the average person.

The most solid reference point I can offer is the mechanical movement of a screw. When we drive a screw into a piece of material, for example like wood, we turn the screwdriver in a clockwise direction. This drives the screw into the wood and away from us. When we "unscrew" it, we turn it in a counterclockwise direction and it moves toward us. The old training the apprentice used to hear is "rightee, tightee, lefty, loosee." This makes its movement easy to remember and is the same dynamic movement that energy follows; clockwise, away from us, and counterclockwise, toward us.

FRICTION, HEAT & RESISTANCE

When energy moves smoothly, there is no *friction*, no *heat* and no *resistance*. When we direct energy and it encounters *friction* or *resistance*, the result is *heat* because the energy doesn't move smoothly and is compresses at the point of *resistance*. *Friction* occurs where *some* movement is accomplished but the movement drags much more slowly than we intend it to which, in turn, also produces *heat*. That *friction* and *resistance* comes as the result of directing energy at someone or something that can't, refuses or is not designed to move. Let's take a look at a few examples.

The simplest example would be when we briskly rub our hands together. This creates *heat* in our hands. Our physical hands essentially resist any change in their structure and so the rubbing creates *friction* which produces *heat*. Many tactile healers do this before they work on someone's body. When contact is made after rubbing the hands together, the compressed energy in the hands is released into the client causing the movement of energy between the healer and the client. However, if the client is averse to receiving the healer's energy, *heat* will remain and build *heat* in both the healer and the client at the point of contact through the *resistance* produced by the client.

Another example might be if we are pushing a car up a hill. The car is dead weight and not likely to move without some outside force. According to Newton's laws, an object at rest will remain so unless acted on by an outside force. As we push, we meet the *resistance* of an immoveable object (the car) which causes *us* to overheat from the *resistance* of the non-flowing energy backing up and causing us to sweat in our body's attempt to cool down. Depending on the mass of the object, it may eventually move if enough energy is applied to overcome its inertia. Since it is *we* who are directing the energy to control the movement, it is *we* who overheat because it compresses in us as a result of the applied energy. We can say the same about lifting weights in the gym. The weights are dead weight resisting our intended movement as *we* are applying the energy to lift them through our attention and direction.

When we scrub a resistant stain on the floor, we produce *heat* from the *friction* and the *resistance* of movement from the stain again creates compression and *heat* is created in both the rub site and in our body.

If we saw a piece of wood, two inanimate objects, the wood and the saw, will generate heat between the wood and the saw *and* in us. Our directed and compressed energy is what is *resisted,* creating *friction* and *heat.*

When applying energy to an inanimate object, pushing a car, scrubbing a stain, lifting weights, it will be *we* who produce the *heat* due to our application the compressing of energy through the object's *resistance* to movement. When we apply energy to *another person,* the natural laws operate the same way but are mitigated by each person's attention. Remember, energy follows thought. Let's look at different examples.

When six people are evenly distributed in a tug-of-war, the immoveable object is the rope. The *resistance* to movement is felt by all six people, three on either side. Here there is little or no *friction.* However, each trio will generate *heat* as a result of acting against the other trio's application of energy and attention pulling in the opposing direction.

Lastly, we have a more complicated example if only because there are many physical and emotional interplays. Two people having sex would create many enabling and inhibiting factors. There is only one aspect of that that I would like to cover here. Suffice it to say here that there will either be, whether conscious or not, the tendency to welcome or resist each other's energy.

When the energy is welcomed, there may be a modicum of *heat* generated due to the process of aligning with each other's differing energy types past their natural physical *resistance.* However, if there is difficulty in that alignment or if one of the participants is resistant or unable to let go into the orgasm, one or both participants will feel the *resistance* and the energy will compress in one or both creating heat, possibly leading to sweating.

MAGNETISM, ATTRACTION & GRAVITY

Thus far we have spoken of characteristics primarily related to the *resistance* of space and matter to movement. Now, we will speak of what *creates* movement.

All matter contains a combination of energy and substance. The same can be said of energy. Whether all is alive or not is still being debated by all the world's greatest philosophers and will be until we cease to exist as we do. Suffice it to say that all matter, even if to a small degree, contains energy and energy, by itself, is the proponent of movement. Conversely, all energy, even if to a small degree, contains some semblance of matter and matter, by itself, is the proponent of stillness. Also added to these "axioms," is the assumption by many that anything that moves has "life." Since all matter contains *some* energy and vice versa, we must assume that all *is* living, even if only to a small degree. Whether or not that "life" must be enlivened through having consciousness is a subject for a much longer and protracted debate elsewhere.

The "life" or energy contained in matter is a varied but perpetual proponent for the change of its state. Since there are no absolutes, all is in a constant state of change or movement between matter and energy. As matter displays the quality of *resistance* and immovability, energy displays the quality of movement and *attraction*. That movement or *attraction* gives all matter the quality of possessing *gravity*. That *gravity* can be the tremendous force that "inhabits" the Earth, or it can be a miniscule force that "inhabits" a grain of sand. All matter has some quantum of *gravity*. Let's take a look at the dynamic of its actions.

If we dump the mercury that inhabits a thermometer, we find that if the wandering beads come close enough to each other, they will exhibit an *attraction* that pulls their separated parts together as one.

An asteroid or any other celestial body traveling through the universe will also tend to grow in size by attracting space debris and smaller bodies to themselves and creating more mass through the *attraction* created by *gravity*. The same would occur with our Moon if it did not have the centrifugal force created by her orbit around us. The centrifugal force counters or *resists* the *gravitational attraction* produced by the *Earth*. With no orbit or centrifugal force, she would literally "fall" to Earth through the pull of *gravity*. The same dynamic can be seen when we observe electrons circling the proton and neutron contained in an atom.

Let's change the consistency of matter a little bit and see what happens. Remember we said that all matter contains some energy, and all energy contains some matter? Why? Because some matter has more mass and is denser than other matter. This would mean the *resistance* to movement would be different between different substances. So, if we have a hunk of lead and a cotton ball, the *resistance* to movement would be more profound in lead than it would be in a cotton ball. Now, picture both the hunk of lead and the cotton ball moving through space. When they came into close proximity to each other, which one would be more likely to be pulled toward the other? Yes, the cotton ball. Why? Because it has less mass or density and is more easily moved than the hunk of lead. So, in our simple example we can see that the strength or *attraction* created by *gravity* is most dependent on its mass and density. The larger or more dense the object, the more *gravity* it exerts. The smaller or less dense it is, the less *gravity* it exerts.

In these examples we can see that *gravity* only exerts a pull or an *attraction* and in one direction. When we speak of *magnetism,* a magnet can exert an *attraction and a repulsion* depending on its orientation.

Natural magnets are comprised of the elements iron, nickel and cobalt. Their force is formed within the Earth's core when these elements come together comprising molten magnetite and then harden in line with the earth's magnetic field. Over millions of years these hardened composites rise to the Earth's surface and become available to us through the movement of our tectonic plates and appear on the surface as lodestone; a natural substance possessing a magnetic field. The majority of magnets today are artificial and created by passing an electric current through coiled wire resulting in the creation of an electromagnetic field.

The force field around a natural magnet is formed by the alignment of the electron spin in each of the three elements in line with the Earth's magnetic field. In artificial magnets, the Earth's field is imitated by passing an electric current through coiled wire windings which also aligns the spin of the electrons.

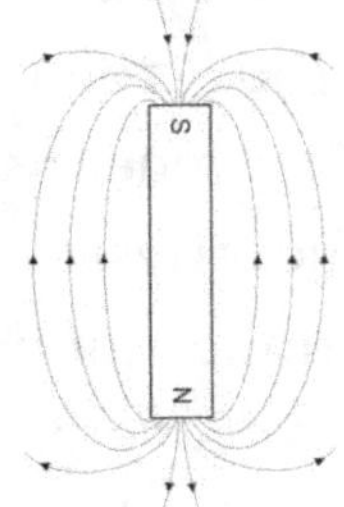

When a magnet is formed, either naturally or artificially, each end of the magnet aligns the electrons differently creating a magnetic field or a *dipole*. This field organizes and radiates from a negative charge at one end toward a positive charge on the other. In a natural magnet, the strength of the field will depend in the amount of magnetic material incorporated into the magnet. The Earth has a tremendous amount of magnetic material contained in its core resulting in a very strong planetary field. In an artificial magnet the strength will depend on the current and the amount of wire coils.

The Earth radiates similarly to the preceding bar magnet diagram. However, her polar correspondence with it is the opposite of what we might think. The north magnetic pole of our bar magnet actually

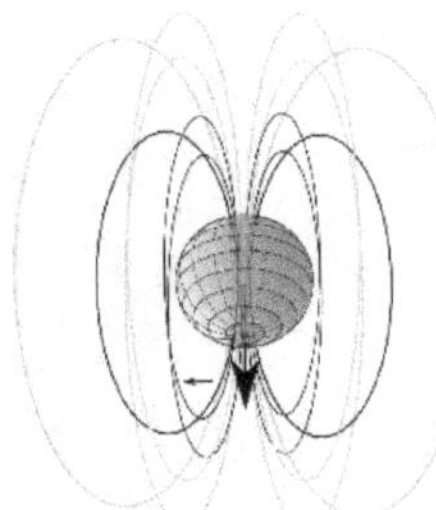

coordinates to our Earth's south pole and the south pole of the bar magnet actually coordinates with the Earth's north pole. The Earth's magnetic field and the direction of its field moves *externally* from south to the north and internally down through the center core from the Earth's north pole to her south pole. Since our bodies resonate as matter or earth, we can assume that the energy flow of our *etheric* aura will work in the same manner: down from the crown through our core down and past our root center (clockwise) and then out from the feet and up and around us (counterclockwise) returning to our crown center. This directional flow provides an energy dedicated to building and maintaining the physical structure and integrity of our body. Please understand that the *etheric* aura is only one of seven types of energy fields that surround our body and corresponds only to the tangible aspects of our body's construction, maintenance and regeneration.

The last necessity that is relative to our practice and understanding is that it has been discovered that the human body contains seven grams of iron mostly posited in our blood (hemoglobin), our bones and the sphenoid/ethmoid sinus complex. This largely accounts for our ability to generate a magnetic field and to sense direction by instinctually perceiving the Earth's magnetic field. This mechanism of recognition is still a mystery to our scientific community.

Part 2

AWARENESS

PERCEPTION, DISCRIMINATION & SUBTLETY

So far, we've talked about dynamics related to physics and natural law. They exemplify the natural laws that we must work with and through as we inhabit our physical bodies. Recognizing and applying these dynamics in how we live our lives is part of a much larger understanding and more progressive process which grows almost solely out of our own experiences and our assessments of their meaning as related to first, our survival while ultimately leading to our spiritual growth. That process of growing awareness goes through steps that utilize *perception* and *discrimination* leading to an increasing subtlety of their use. Our growth is dependent upon our ability to develop a sequential state of awareness where one state *cannot* be addressed or accomplished without completing the level that comes before. To understand this process more clearly, we can take a look at *Maslow's Hierarchy of Needs*. The levels of awareness that are worked through are *survival needs, safety, belonging, esteem* and lastly, *actualization*. Each of these levels requires an awareness wider than the individual's current state of perception in order to progress to a more subtle level of consciousness.

SURVIVAL - *Survival needs* consist primarily of the tangible messages we receive directly from our body. In this level of perception our attention is limited to focusing solely *within* our body and its sensations. It includes hunger, thirst, recovering from physical injury and freedom from pain. Once these issues have been sufficiently addressed our focus lets these issues go and our focus broadens slightly past our bodily sensations to the narrow peripheral space around us in our immediate environment. This focus expands into highlighting aspects of our *safety* which are representative of how our physical body interacts with our immediate environment above and beyond our inner sensations. With this, our circle of attention is made just a little wider.

SAFETY - Our *safety* concerns involve influences that come from *outside* of the body that we may need to compensate for so as not to be either injured or thrown off balance. These may include preventing ourselves from falling in a hole, tripping on the curb, being assaulted by an animal, being hit by a bus, being caught in the rain, hitting our head on a low branch, bumping into another person or any other external circumstance that might injure or influence us in a way that interferes with our expected or healthy living circumstances. To prevent these influences our attention must go beyond our internal sensations and feelings and attend the peripheral environment for situations that might cause a problem.

For *survival* and *safety* concerns *instinct* comes into play. *Instinct* is the body's reaction to an internal state or externally generated movement. There is *no thought* involved. The action is automatic. Let's look at a few examples.

In bodily *survival* reactions we can see *instinct* operating in either an innate revulsion to a certain type of food which might be harmful to us or an urge *for* a certain type of food that might be needed for proper nutrition. Relative to *safety*, we can see an automatic reaction to a ball that is thrown at us so we either catch it or duck, so we don't get hit by it.

Over eons of evolution, we've had endless circumstances training us into incorporating automatic reactions into our movements that enable behaviors that are self-preserving to our species. These have become so familiar to us that we don't even realize when they are occurring.

Once we become comfortable and confident in handling our immediate environment, our focus changes from *what is in* our environment to what it is that we might *want* from our environment. Our focus now broadens even wider toward forming wishes and wants *from* our environment. This expands to seeking *belonging* cues from the environment and the people we find in it. In this our evolving *perception* becomes much more dominant.

BELONGING – Our need for *belonging* utilizes our *perception* in more of a two-way framework. Rather than focusing on only what we want to push away, we expand our focus to what we want to pull towards ourselves. This requires a new type of thinking. Rather than being reactive to external stimuli, we now move toward more of an internal assessment utilizing time and our past and current circumstances. We then incorporate past, present and future in our deliberations. Not only does our focus become wider, but now our comprehension takes on the broader dimension of time. This in itself is an expansion of our *awareness* beyond our immediate feelings and circumstances.

Although there is *safety* in numbers, *belonging* offers much more than just protection. When we sense others following the same processes and paths as we do there arises in us a sense of comradery, slightly reducing our mistrust of the outside world. Everything is no longer seen as a threat. We feel we might have an ally and that we might have a place in the world that might value what we have to offer.

Finding common ground with others gives us a sense of validity in our choices through receiving the real or imagined approval of others. We feel that we are not alone and that others may be facing some of the same challenges that we are. This encourages us to be more open to others if only to find a better way of dealing with our own life circumstances. This reduces the stress involved in feeling challenged or alone in accomplishing our *survival* and assuring our *safety*.

As we realize the sympatico we have with others in selected areas of common interest, we begin to look for people who have a wider array of similar interests with us. We look for a deeper connection of similar values and perceptions. The recognition we receive from others now becomes apparent to us as a need and we start to strive to receive this from others. This recognition has a new quality and is called *esteem*.

ESTEEM – As we do our activities advancing and maintaining our career, survival and life plans, we learn skills and hopefully become proficient in them. In acquiring these proficiencies, we often gain qualifications, recognition, prestige and the admiration and respect of others. This broadens our understanding of how we affect and are affected by others and, hopefully, we become aware of how that acknowledgement influences us. When we feel those positive vibes directed at us it gives us a sense of pride and a "social score" akin to merit and value in the eyes of others. This merit and value can be termed *esteem*.

In reaping *esteem*, our perceived positive *self-worth* blossoms into a growing contentment on the social stage. If we have been raised to feel that we have positive *self-worth* in our family and its expansion on to the social stage, confidence and modesty will assume a position in our character. If we have been raised feeling negative *self-worth* in our family, that too expands to the world, and we become beset with the desperate pursuit of positive acknowledgement exhibiting *esteem* through compensatory behavior.

Acquiring *esteem* is again an even more subtle level of sensitivity above and beyond the levels of *survival, safety* and *belonging*. Generally, when we reach the level of *esteem* and acquire the confidence and modesty brought by emotional maturity, actualization has been accomplished. That is, there are no more contingencies of subtlety that must be passed through. According to Maslow we have reached the peak of our hierarchy. All that comes after that is simply more experience and enjoyment of our position in life. All these levels exhibit a growing sense of awareness based on more and more subtle comprehensions of life and its consequences.

In advancing through *Maslow's Hierarchy of Needs* we can see that each level requires us to gain a deeper and more subtle sensitivity of ourselves and our interrelationship with the world around us. I have used the hierarchy because it shows definite benchmarks of accomplishment that the average person can comprehend. Maslow's hierarchy is a very solid analogy to the process that is needed to advance "up" through the *chakras* in maturity and awareness. With this in mind, let's expand on into my chart of *Sequential Progressive Awareness*.

SEQUENTIAL PROGRESSIVE AWARENESS

On first examining the chart you will notice that there are no definite plateaus where you can recognize a large difference from the step that came before as in *Maslow's Hierarchy of Needs*. Each step has a small and subtle change in our *perception* that marks our growth and enables our progression on to the next "level." Our circle of awareness grows ever wider with the realization that our world is infinitely more than simply our *perception* of it. Please also notice that at a certain point of *awareness* that our method of handling the changes that we feel comes to a crossroad. We either do our best to resist the changes and bury our recognition of them (left column) or we choose to allow them to permeate us and continue on with the natural flow of circumstances based on our choices (right column).

Before we move on, please reread the chart with special attention to how you feel as you comprehend the shifts and what subtleties you are able to perceive in your life and how you deal with them.

No sensitivity and no awareness.
Anxious and uncomfortable but not aware of feeling so. Exhibits a "knee jerk" reaction with a lack of awareness of doing so.
Anxious and uncomfortable *with* an awareness of feeling so (A&U w/A of feeling so). Still exhibits a "knee jerk" reaction with a lack of awareness of doing so.
(A&U w/A of feeling so). Exhibits a "knee jerk" reaction *with* an awareness of doing so.
(Crossroads for choosing method of coping – Left column is "pushing the river" and right column is "going with the flow.")

Consciously or unconsciously *obsesses and distracts* with activities in order to cloak the anxious and uncomfortable feelings.	(A&U w/A of feeling so) Possesses enough awareness of their reactivity to *choose the type of reaction* to exhibit.
Feels anxious and uncomfortable no longer with the awareness of feeling so. *Drawn to substances that deaden the senses* masking and suppressing the anxiety and uncomfortablility.	(A&U w/A of feeling so). Aware and detached enough to recognize that they can *choose to react or not.*
As tolerance level is reached, the substance is no longer at an effective enough intensity to deaden the senses. Anxiety & uncomfortablility "bleed through." Increasing the dosage of distraction only serves to increase the tolerance level thereby spiraling the resurfacing anxiety & uncomfortablility sooner and sooner.	(A&U w/A of feeling so). Aware and detached enough to recognize that they can *choose to remove themselves from the circumstances creating the stress and/or plan prevention for future involvements.*
Discomfort becomes intolerable. The desire for oblivion and suicide may be considered.	(A&U w/A of feeling so). Aware and detached enough to ask *what is the cause* of these feelings?
	(A&U w/A of feeling so). Aware and detached enough to ask could it be that they might *be "in sync"* with the feelings of someone else?
	(A&U w/A of feeling so). Aware and detached enough to accept the possibility that they may be *tuning into someone else's feelings* and considering the possibility that what they are feeling

	might not be of their own making.
	Aware and detached enough to ask if they are doing or contributing something that *enables their receptivity* to someone else's feelings.
	Aware and detached enough to ask if their action somehow *fosters the other person's feelings and emissions.*
	Aware and detached enough to ask if they can somehow *alter or morph what the other person is feeling and emitting.*

After we have carefully assessed our own feelings and thoughts, we may likely be able to pinpoint where we are in the progression of our growing awareness. As compared to Maslow's format, we can see that each of these changes are much more subtle indeed and are not easily recognizable except through a meticulous scrutiny of ourselves. Many people are not even aware of their own thoughts let alone what they may be feeling. This kind of scrutiny requires a detachment that the average person is usually *incapable* of doing so due to a lack of experience or training by parents or guardians. Self-analysis is not a common skill taught to westerners as we tend to focus more on what the world is doing or expecting of us. This style of focus tends to cloak our *intuition*. What is even further from our consciousness is how we may be contributing to how others may be acting or reacting as a function of our actions.

Spiritual growth is a *very* slow process and may take many years to expand our *perception* to include the wider subtleties of life. Everyone's experience will be different, which may account for why some people evolve faster than others.

Relative to the more commonly held view of *chakras*, they are not simply destinations or places to get to and then reside. The borders of their influence are very fluid, undefined and not easily discriminated from each other. They have hazy and composite points of perspective that interrelate in ways that may connect in ways more subtle than what we might be able to distinguish or comprehend.

In our reaching these points of perspective there are no guarantees that we will remain in our accomplished "mindsets" as there are myriads of influences that may trip us up causing us to tumble back into our prior and more limited mental and emotional patterns. We may also add more difficulty to our ability to discriminate where we are as the *chakras* often work together in combinations foreign to human logic. A simple analogy might be to compare what we need in our *awareness* to comprehending 3D chess. Simultaneous multilevel awareness is one of the most difficult perspectives to achieve, let alone, maintain.

The primary "activator" for the *chakras* is the *kundalini* which is also known as the "serpent's fire." In the larger majority of humans it resides, sleeping, in our *root center* and is only awakened by consciously opening the doors to the subtleties of a growing awareness. Its symbolism can be found in the center staff of the *caduceus* as it is entwined with polarized but balanced serpents and eventually gaining the wings of consciousness as it "ascends" through the *crown chakra*. In crude and tangible examples, we might compare it to the mercury ascending up a glass thermometer or our attempting to ring the bell in a carnival circus hammer, although, many of us may be way too young to have experienced the latter.

In our discussions of the *chakras*, I will discuss most of them in tangible terms as best as I am able, but it must be understood that as we move to the "higher" *chakras*, our discussion must become much more subtle and less easily explained or understood.

Before we move on, I would like to clarify some terms in the way that I understand them and perhaps differently than the average person might. This will keep us on the same page as we endeavor to distinguish the meanings and influences of each of the *chakras* and how we can relate to them. These terms are *awareness, perception* and *discrimination*.

Awareness – *Awareness* is regarded as a noun and the state of being *aware*. *Aware* comes from the Old English *gewaer* meaning to be watchful and vigilant. Documentation of its use first appeared in 1545. It suggests a quality of being *passive*. Other words that might be used are listening, attentive, observant, looking to, taking notice and being wary. These are all concepts of becoming conscious of an event or of something or someone coming into someone's sphere of notice. It is *passive* because no action is taken. It may be the triggering of one of our senses. It is becoming conscious of an occurrence that is allowed to proceed without our interference, analysis or judgement.

Perception – *Perception* is regarded as a verb. This makes it *active*. It was first seen c. 1300 as *perceiven* originally in the Latin *percipere* from *per*, thoroughly, and *capere*, "to grasp, to take." So, the grasping or taking involves our *active* approach. Other words that might be used are apprehend, catch, learn, comprehend, obtain, gather, seize and take possession of. It is *active* because these activities require a directed participation. They may trigger our senses but may also to a lesser extent involve our *intuition*. The occurrence is proceeding with our direction and participation.

Discrimination – *Discrimination* is an *active* verb deriving from the Latin *discriminatus*, which was first encountered in 1620 and is the past participle of *discriminare* meaning to divide or separate. Other words with a similar meaning would be to set apart or distribute. It is further derived from *discernere* and broken down to *dis*, meaning "off or away" and *cernere* meaning to "distinguish, separate, sift." For our purposes, we can say that *discriminating* is an active mental function equating to *sorting*.

With these meanings under our belt, let's now move on to each of the *chakras*, their correspondences and how we should "associate" with them.

Part 3

THE CHAKRAS

In the same fashion that we have nerve plexus' conjuncting at various areas in the body, we also have energy plexus' that overlay those junctures. In metaphysical traditions these areas are called *chakras*. The word *chakra* comes from the Sanskrit meaning wheel. Hence, the points in the body where the *chakras* are positioned are also called vortexes. Since sound, light and energy travels in cycles, these serve as good examples for how energy moves in the *chakras*; also spinning in cycles. The faster they spin, the higher the frequency. The slower they spin, the lower the frequency. In the same way that it can be determined which way the energy will flow through an electromagnet (by changing the polarity); we also have the capability to determine the direction the energy will flow cycling in the *chakra* (projecting or receiving). Suffice it to say for now that if the spin, from our vantage point, is counterclockwise, the energy will be moving toward us. If moving clockwise, projecting or away from us. Hence, we can say it is moving inward or outward. For example, to take this concept further; when we are speaking, the energy will flow clockwise and away from us (outward). When we are listening, the energy will be flowing counterclockwise and toward us (inward).

The *chakras* are "connected" to many different references, qualities and aspects of all life. These correspondences are endless since they permeate and include every aspect of human existence. To delineate them here would be a monumental task that can be covered better by the multitude of books currently on the market. My aim here is to describe the "head space" and cognitive perception of an individual who may potentially "operate" on each of the levels. To this end I have endeavored to build an awareness gage of an individual's ability to perceive through our previous chart of *Sequential Progression of Awareness*.

Before covering each level, it's important to understand the building effect of moving from one center to the next. To do so requires us to move through them *sequentially*. That is, we cannot "skip" one center to move to the next. What is contained in each center must necessarily be ingested and integrated in order to comprehend and use what is being offered through the next center. In a sense, we can call this a chain of command. To skip the experience needed to develop the capacity inherent to the next sequential level in order to "move up the ranks" leaves us at a deficit for what must be understood before we can apply our skills effectively. In business, skipping levels might be called the "Peter Principle" which is where an individual is promoted beyond his capabilities and is unable to function effectively in the tasks to be tackled. In a grosser comparison, we might say that one who crawls needs to learn to walk before they can run.

Additionally, when I describe "where" the chakra or center is located in the body, I will give the location to which it has traditionally been applied but we must realize that when a center is actively assimilated and integrated, that area will extend outward. How far it extends or, more appropriately, how intensely the field may be developed depends on the maturity and awareness of the person the field emanates from. Its emanation is a function of both the projective and receptive capacities of the individual. So, a person who has only recently begun to work with the center may only appear to resonate within a mere point in the body, where a person who has integrated the qualities may "broadcast" well past the borders of his body. We should also realize that though a person may have assimilated and integrated the energies of that center, it is not a permanent condition and that the individual may easily regress toward a prior more limiting perspective of life based on grosser desires and the gained abilities may go dormant until the perceptive state is again achieved. The only difference between one who has lost capacity and one who has just gained is the ease and speed with which that center is then again resonated with. Understand that when I say resonated with, I am referring to returning to a state of perception more broadly centered than the center the individual has recently "graduated" from.

THE LANDSCAPE

Although there are seven *chakras* that are commonly known, each of them will operate slightly differently when our point of reference ascends in *awareness* to the next *chakra* above. For example, when we operate from strictly a *root center* perspective, the way the *chakra* will be utilized will be from a perspective that strictly deals with *survival*. However, when we are more centered in the *sacral center*, the *root center* will be utilized in ways that are more expansive than just for *survival*. In this way the corresponding energies will manifest differently. Hence, if we operate strictly from a *root center* perspective, the color most associated with it may be red. But if our perspective operates more from a *sacral center* orientation, the color associated with the *root center* may adjust to an alternate color symbolizing the inclusion of other energies. In this way we can see that each center, relative to color, may resonate differently depending on which *chakra* we are oriented from. This will give us a partial understanding why some scriptures hold that there are forty-nine levels rather than just the expected seven of common knowledge. Color is then only one of the dimensions that can be attributed to their combined energies.

The most fundamental orientation of the centers presents an alternation of polarities as our *kundalini* spirals up the *Sushumna* channel (*kundalini* pathway

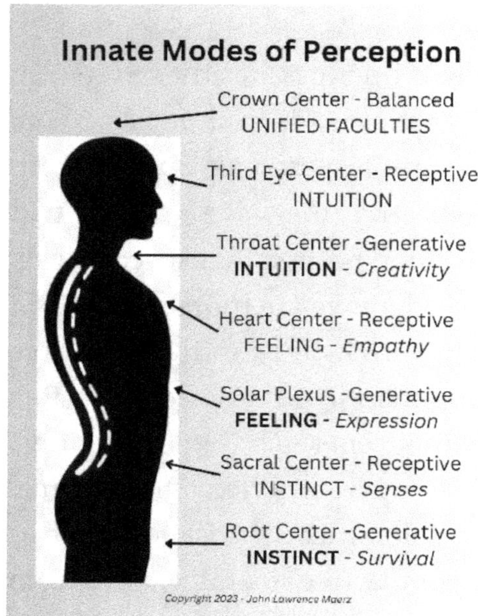

and center staff of the *caduceus*). The *root center* is generative, the *sacral center* is receptive, the *solar plexus* is generative, the *heart center* is receptive, the *throat center* is generative, the *third eye* is receptive, and the *crown center* is balanced in universal manifestation.

In the diagram we can also see that the *chakras* are paired with the use of *instinct, feeling* and *intuition*. The *root center* generates from *instinct* and the *sacral center* "listens" to it through the *senses*. The *solar plexus* generates *feeling* and the *heart center* "listens" to it through *empathy*. The *throat center* generates *creativity* and the third eye "listens" to it though *intuition* and the *crown center* "resolves" the polarity through aligning with universal manifestation.

As our point of orientation rises through the *chakras*, the use of *instincts, feelings* and *intuition* will be applied differently depending on our *current* state of spiritual maturity. In this way our *instincts, feelings* and *intuition* will also be perceived differently depending on our conscious point of orientation (*chakra* point of perspective).

THE MODES: INSTINCT, FEELING & INTUITION

There are three modes of operation humans use to deal with the world. They are *instinct, feeling* and *intuition*. As seen in the previous figure, they operate through the *chakras* in pairs. Each lower one *acts* and the next upper one *listens* alternating *active* and *receptive* as they move up the *kundalini*. The last one, the *crown center*, produces unified *gestalt* for the whole system. Let's move on to where *instinct* comes from.

INSTINCT

First, *instinct* comes from eons of evolution in our *species* unconscious. Second, it occurs *automatically* as a function of being solely connected to and generated by the tangible body. That is, it is *not* part of, nor does it need, any conscious awareness for it to occur. Through incarnating we "inherit" a body that is constructed by a specific genetic lineage that includes a *survival instinct* that has evolved through eons of species experience. It is in the DNA. This is *not* a component of our spiritual *awareness*. It is totally tangible, and it "comes" with the body we choose to inhabit. It is one of the things that grounds us and reinforces our spirit's connection into the physical plane. When we die, it is also one of the qualities that is shed along with the body. It is part of our spiritual growth only in as much as it exists as a starting point for our need to identify with more than just the body and the tangible world. The point I endeavor to make here is that *instinct* is *separate* from our consciousness. It develops solely through the functioning of matter. With this being said, let's look at understanding its dynamic.

The *root center* simply responds to *instinct* and acts as a result of an inner impulse toward *survival* while the *sacral center* listens to it and is drawn into aligning with the natural flow of order to gain an edge in nature. So, it occurs *only* through impulse or reaction. Thinking takes no part in its action except maybe as an afterthought. Its process of occurrence is *not* understood by the average person and assumed to have *feeling* at its core which it does not. It is automatic and occurs *involuntarily*. *Feeling* might generated as a result of its occurrence.

If we were to ask someone to define *instinct*, most people would say that it's a "gut feeling." If we were to ask them in terms of animals, most people would say that it is something that most animals "just know" pertinent to their *survival*. Most people don't make the connection between human *instinct* and animal *instinct*. However, they are the same. Why? Because, whether we accept it or not, we too are animals. The next question to ask would be, do animals think before they act? The answer would generally be no. We find very few species seeming to possess the power of thought. Humans are essentially the only animals that have the capacity to think. This would tell us that the *action* that results from *instinct* does not use or require thinking. It simply "happens" as an *action* that is devoid of any mental interference. How do we know this? Let's look at a simple example.

If we are sitting at a table and swiftly turn from one side to the other knocking a glass off the surface, what happens? Quick as a flash, we snap into action grabbing the glass before it hits the floor. Did we first think, "I must grab the glass before it hits the floor?" No. We simply reacted with a quick movement. If we thought about it before we moved, the glass would have shattered on the floor long before we sprang into *action*. In another example, if we made a fast movement toward an animal, would it first think, "I don't want to get hit" or would it take a swipe at us defending itself against aggression and then swiftly move away? Its *reaction* would be almost instantaneous. These *actions* in our animalistic history go back hundreds if not thousands of generations and have become inbred into every type of living creature. So much so that defensive and survival action has been incorporated into our genes and DNA. These *actions* happen without thought. There is simply a *reaction* to what we perceive as possibly being a danger to our well-being. It is literally inbred. We've become trained into becoming defensive toward anything that intrudes into the familiarity of our space. No thought. Just *action*. Now as humans, our threatening situations may move more slowly where we may have the opportunity to think before we act, perhaps like a mugging or car accident.

But generally, we have the same "snap to it" capacity to act defensively as do other species of animals.

Things get a little confusing when humans talk about a *gut instinct*. What we really mean is a *gut feeling* rather than actual *instinct*. *Instinct* is purely a *survival* mechanism connected to the *base center* and *sacral center chakras*. There is neither *feeling* nor thinking involved. Additionally, the *base center* is only involved in tangible *action* for *survival* while the *sacral center* is involved with *listening* for the cues in nature that will provide that *survival*. *Feeling* is a projective capacity connected to the *solar plexus chakra* and made functional through facilitation of the *lower mind's* ability to discriminate differences in *feeling*.

FEELING

So, what is *feeling*? It is a movement of energy through us that we perceive in waves. It literally grows from a ripple to an ocean wave, peaks to intensity and then subsides just as gradually. Generally, *feelings* have little or no distinguishable beginnings or endings. There are no sharp starts or stops unless adrenalin is involved. They usually grow from a miniscule imperceivable change and register at and through our threshold of awareness and eventually retreat in the same way. *Instinctual actions* or *reactions* come from a sudden or sharp occurrence while *feelings* grow slowly, peak and fall away just as slowly. They teach us more subtly and precisely how to discriminate the movement of energy. The type of *feelings* we perceive are determined and categorized by way of our experiences and the mental judgments we attach to them as we experience them.

Since the *lower mind* is centered in the *solar plexus chakra*, it is what we use to classify the *feelings* we may experience. When we recognize a *feeling* rising within us, the *lower mind* simultaneously pairs the *feeling* with the judgment of what we are experiencing in the moment. That same *feeling* may be characterized in two different ways depending on whether the *feeling* we are experiencing occurs in anticipating a situation we find pleasurable or distasteful. As an example, if we are facing a test of some sort, what we *feel* might be characterized as dread. Conversely, if we are anticipating something that will be pleasurable, we might characterize it as excitement. Both these *feelings* are likely to be felt physically in the *solar plexus* as butterflies. If you're honest with yourself, you can check your own history of *feelings* and see the similarities between what we are anticipatory about. Both dread and excitement will generally register in the body the same way. What differs will be if we are either attracted to or avoidant of the situation.

Feeling emanates as a projection from the *solar plexus* and is perceived in the *heart center* through *empathy*. Again, sequentially, like the *root center* and *sacral center*, the *solar plexus chakra* generates it, and the *heart chakra* listens for it. When we listen for it and we "hear" it, it is called *empathy*. I will cover it here but only briefly as I will go much more in depth during our discussion of the *heart center chakra* later.

When we *empathize feelings*, we pick them up and absorb them *involuntarily*. Additionally, most of us are unaware of picking up and absorbing them. When we do, we simply lack discrimination and assume that they are of our own making and automatically *react* to them. In doing so we ultimately have an ancillary effect on the body: changing blood pressure, tightening muscles, protective posturing, etc.

The unconditional part of the *heart chakra's* activities is that we absorb and process *all* the *feelings* within proximity to us, especially, if we are sensitive and lack boundaries. The key to understanding this is that our absorption is *involuntary*. Although we listen with the *heart chakra*, we rarely "hear" what's being emitted as something foreign to our normal demeanor. Our lack of discrimination causes many problems in our interpersonal relationships. The point to be understood here is that the *heart chakra* is totally *empathetic* and *receptive* while the *solar plexus* is *active* and projective. More on *empathy* later.

INTUITION

Intuition is a horse of a completely different color. So far, *instinct* involves and affects the body directly and *feelings* have more of an ancillary effect on the body that is not easily recognizable. *Intuition*, by comparison, has virtually *no effect* on the body. It is something perceived on a completely different level. First, it is not time constrained like *instinct* or *feelings*. Both *instinct* and *feelings* have a beginning and an ending. *Intuition* is perceived in its totality. That is, it is perceived with the past, present and future having occurred at the same time. It is a perception that is experienced in its completeness on many levels all at once. In this, there is no mental component as with the *solar plexus*. Mental movement requires a sequence of events to function. *Intuition* is free of that. Second, because of its absence of time, it is perceived in a flash or as a lightning bolt. Hence, as a complete picture. Its closest analogy is a dream. When we try to fit it into a mental sequence, we almost always lose it.

The *throat center* uses the dynamics of *intuition* through projection. It is most effective when we see our objective as already completed in its most fully integrated form. 100% is easy. 99% or less is a bear. It harbors no contingencies. The *third eye* or *Ajna center* is like a TV receiver. It manifests the *intuitive* experience simply as a "knowing" in full color and spiritual reality. Whether we comprehend it or not is a different story. Working with *intuition* will be discussed in more depth when I cover the *throat* and *third eye centers* later.

NAVIGATING THE CENTERS

As we move up the *kundalini*, each mode becomes more subtle and less tangible. The *root center chakra* is completely tangible and is there to anchor us into the physical body when we incarnate. The *solar plexus* is our first stop in reaching for a different mode of operation more than just the tangible. Our crossroads toward manifesting the spirit through the physical body is the *heart center* which is our species' current center of evolution. Although the *heart center* is our species' nexus for change, many souls don't evolve past the *solar plexus* in this lifetime. Some don't even surpass the *sacral center*. Some make it all the way to the *crown center*. Please remember also that we can fall back as easily as we move forward. Each person's lessons are different and vary in depth, intensity and integration. In this light we should never think because someone is working on a lower center that they are less evolved than we are.

An additional point must be understood. Though we may be primarily residential in one of the centers, we may operate intermittently from different centers at different times depending on the situations that we're dealing with. For example, we may at times show brilliance in our mental and reasoning powers that are developed efficiently but still primarily operate with deficiency in our emotional coping. That is, we may manifest action in the scientific realm of the world with expertise and proficiency yet react poorly in our personal relationships from a lower center perspective if our emotional *self-worth* is at low tide.

Nothing is consistent, written in stone, guaranteed or "permanent" in terms of our growth being automatic or "fated." All is dependent on our choices and our willingness toward acting with spiritual maturity. Hence, all is dependent on our attention, perseverance and diligence relative to our lessons, beliefs and highest personal standards.

THE ROOT CENTER

Survival & Pleasure

Modes of Operation: *Generative, Instinctual and sense based & internally cognizant only*

The *root center*, or *Muladhara* in Sanskrit, is located at the entry point of the vagina on a female and the position of the prostate on the male. This is also where the individual's essence resides until it is called upon by our spirit to grow toward spiritual maturity. This is in the bottom part of the bodily trunk and where a reservoir of energy called the *kundalini* resides. It is the starting point for the circulation or flow of our spirit energy up through the other *chakras*.

If we were to isolate the *root center* from its integration with the other centers, this center would be solely focused on relieving the stress created by our necessities for *survival*. To this end it is actively mobilized toward the acquisition of food, shelter and perpetuation of the species. It is almost totally *unconscious* and operates through *instinct* where there is little or no *awareness* of anything other than our encountered lack of *survival* needs associated with feeling comfortable and sated. Our objective is *unconsciously* programmed toward recreating the conditions that were present before we exited the womb. In this "headspace" there is only a purely selfish orientation directed toward our own comfort and pleasure. We could say that this might be a parallel focus to that of Freud's *id*. From the point of view of the *root center*, any sense of *consciousness* above and beyond that *awareness* will be completely absent. The only *awareness* present is the feeling of separation from whatever it is that will neutralize felt pain or bodily discomfort. To this end, we essentially have *involuntary* urges toward being physically sated in every way. Its prime directive is pleasure and freedom from any imposing tension or restriction.

This center deals with the physiological needs corresponding to Maslow's first level of his *Hierarchy of Needs*: breathing, food, water, sex, homeostasis and excretion (Maslow, 1943). Any sexual activity will be *unconsciously* directed toward perpetuation of the species and *consciously* directed toward achieving the pleasure of orgasm. Any partner will suffice. The qualities of the partner are unimportant except for their capacity to enable the facilitation of an orgasm. By itself, the physical orgasm is an almost total but temporary reduction of *physical* tension. The urge is driven by the natural polarity present in the "separation of the sexes." The physical bond that is created, if any, might only be considered "future insurance" for the satisfying of their desires. Even so, no *awareness* of the future will be present.

The only *awareness* of feeling is internal and that of comfort. In terms of our survival and our animal side, our comfort within our own body is the only measure of feeling connected to the *root center*. Those who have a "disconnect" or a discomfort with the way they feel within their own body will have difficulties in creating physical relations with members of the opposite sex. Those who appear to possess an "animal magnetism" are generally more comfortable with but less aware of their own sexuality thereby producing a much larger component of sex hormones than those who have been "unsuccessful" in the acquisitions of partners for physical release. Indiscriminate choices for sexual activity are indicative of an individual operating solely from the *root center*. *Root center* activity operates almost exclusively in the moment. There is, essentially, no planning or regard, let alone *awareness*, of consequences except an *instinct* toward the relief of physical stress. Their actions are totally *reactive*. Any planning for future endeavors, if any are apparent, would be a function of higher centers. In addition to the sex drive, adrenaline and the "fight or flight" *instinct* are also connected to the *root center* and are a product of eons of experience accumulated in our species "memory" in defending ourselves.

For the male whose spiritual development is primarily centered in the *root center*, his focus would totally be on his survival and pleasure with no concern or consideration of anyone else. Food and shelter would occupy his primary focus with comfort, pleasure and the relieving of any tension or stress as his focus after the first issues two have been answered in total.

When it comes to sex, his *unconscious* urge coupled with hormonal influence toward procreating the species would dominate his interaction with females. Consequently, his *conscious* urge would be toward the pleasure of orgasm and relieving the physical tension that accompanies an overwhelming libido. To this end his overtures to the female would include "strutting," projecting domination, preening, and an expectation of the female's submission whether by force or her willing appeasement. Refined behavior would have no place in the exchange except as a learned previous method to acquire satisfaction. His animal magnetism, if he has any, would dominate the interchange and pheromones would emphasize the projection of a strong libido. Unless other centers were involved in his encounters, no fidelity, commitment or female consideration would have any place whatsoever.

For the female whose spiritual development is primarily centered in the *root center*, her focus would totally be on her survival and the need to reproduce with no concern or consideration of anyone else. Food, shelter and an *unconscious* urge toward procreation would occupy her primary focus with comfort, pleasure and the relieving on any tension or pressure as her focus after the first two concerns have been answered.

When it comes to sex, her *unconscious* urge toward reproducing would dominate her interaction with males. Her *conscious* urge would be toward pleasure and seduction toward bringing on the pleasure that accompanies the sexual act and receiving male energy.

For the female whose spirituality is primarily centered in the *root center*, all manner of seduction would saturate her interaction with a male. Every opportunity to be in his space with offers for her availability for a sexual encounter would dominate her action. Her submissiveness would be clearly broadcast along with the appropriate pheromones that indicate her readiness for interaction.

Imbalances in the *root center* would be indistinguishable except through the extremes that the *root center* energies work toward. They would occur as obsessions with pleasure, food, sex and dominance over personal territory. These obsessions would take their form by way of unmitigated aggression. They would truly bring unbridled offense and assault on others exemplifying the worst part of Freud's *id*.

In reference to worldly correspondences, the lowest level of the *root center* color would be red. The *root center* also is representative of the mineral kingdom with its intended evolution toward the *sacral center* and the plant kingdom. The *root center* also corresponds to the Fourth Ray of *Harmony Through Conflict* in Alice Bailey's hierarchy of esoteric and astrological ray energies. The planets Mercury and the Moon are their closest representatives. In the Kabbalah, it equates to Malkuth. The glands most closely associated are the adrenals.

THE SACRAL CENTER
Natural Response

Modes of Operation: *Receptive, Instinctual and sense based & internally and externally cognizant*

The *sacral center,* or the *Swadhisthana* in Sanskrit, is located three inches below the belly button in a line with the "small" of the back. The center itself is inside the body but just in front of the spine. This center is primarily concerned with the natural order of nature and our sense balance in our keeping aligned with it. In the martial arts it is also known as the *Tan Tien* center (pronounced dan cheeyen). Physically, it is the center point of gravity for the entire body. It is also the storage point for *chi* or life energy and considered the lower part of the *triple warmer* as related to Chinese health practices.

As the receptive side of our pair of *instinctual chakras (root & sacral),* the *sacral center* is largely governed through *listening* to our *senses.* In this way we assess our position in the larger scheme of things physically. This *chakra* might be considered to be equivalent to a "tribal" orientation (Ruumet, 2006) only in as much as we may take cues for *survival* from our environment and others in it. In terms of Maslow's *Hierarchy of Needs,* it fulfills the second level of *safety.* It is held from the perspective of what the individual may gain in *survival* from any group they choose to be part of. Even though it might not look totally selfish, it is still part of the *survival* mindset. It is believed that security and well-being can be gained through grouping with others who may have "an edge" over nature contributing to our *safety*. We might say that it exemplifies "safety in numbers."

This level of *awareness* works with reciprocal providing and receiving. Focus on another person is more in terms of them being a vehicle to an end rather than as an individual. In this light most people are viewed "en-masse." The only differences might be when one individual or group has a specific possession or quality that would be seen as, again, giving "an edge" to the purveyor. There is a rudimentary form of *awareness* in listening to their *instinct* through their *senses* but only in terms of what is needed or wanted and how it will affect their *survival* and comfort status.

Sex on this level is selective and is in terms of catharsis relative to our personal needs, taste and tension. The individual who best fits those tastes and qualities with the ability to relieve those personal needs in a preferred way would be sought out and likely retained for future physical pleasure and release. In this way, the individual would attach themselves to the person(s) with their preferred qualities with the idea of them potentially satisfying their specific needs in the future. More evolved relationships may be possible but only as an "accidental" result of these pursuits.

Any group possessing preferred specific qualities would be sought after and joined strictly for the *survival* and pleasure benefits offered by the group.

These would include conventional religion, unions, politics or any other groups focused on their combined social usefulness for the purpose of having the pick of individuals with preferred or needed qualities from a "larger gene pool."

Positioning in any of the groups would be subject to the laws of dominance and Darwin's postulates of *natural selection* and *survival of the fittest*. Here our *senses* are highly employed through listening to the more subtle patterns of nature contrary to the blunt action of the *root center*. Our focus is directed toward the environment rather than toward our internal feelings and individual comfort. In the *sacral center* our *senses* qualify as a set of listening "organs."

Every living thing has its place in the grand scheme of nature. Eons of evolution have refined the stream of rebalancing in nature where all living things follow the natural flow. Listening to our *senses* enables us to tune into that natural flow independent of our preferences and personal idiosyncrasies. In doing so we can align ourselves where nature can assist us in our *survival*. Those of us who do not align with the natural flow do not *survive*. Outliers are removed through *natural section* unless they prove to be a better avenue the for *survival* of the species than what currently exists.

The *sacral* or *Tan Tien center* is the fulcrum point in the human body for physical balance. It also lends itself to being the reservoir and storage point for *chi* as utilized by martial arts, dance and any movements involving physical precision and skill. It is the center in which our *senses* can be developed to a refined point of subtlety.

Our *senses* are tangible receivers grounded in receptive organs that listen to and send interpretable messages about the environment through different modes of perception to the brain. These modes are sight, sound, tactile, smell and taste. They reach out into the environment in a spread of *awareness* that is wider than the inner attention centered in only the *root center*. The *sacral center* and these listening devices keep us aware of the dangers that we encounter around us. It gives us the opportunity to choose to be safe through remaining in balance with the tangible world and its laws. For survival patterns that have evolved over eons, the *senses* and their input remain *unconscious*. We react tangibly through *instinct*. But for situations that are novel and new, our *conscious awareness* is involuntarily triggered toward becoming thoughtfully attentive to the uniqueness of what we receive. We then have an opportunity to assess our *safety* in the environment and make a conscious choice.

Being human, having the capacity for thought makes this possible. However, other creatures in the animal kingdom who don't have the capacity for thought only react purely "unconsciously." The presence of thought does not interfere with their *instinctual* reactions as it does with humans. Hundreds of years developing the power and skill of thought has superseded and eclipsed the availability and quickness of our once unconscious *instinct*. In dangerous situations we may then hesitate, thereby risking our *survival*.

Of late, many more people have moved into nature and are living "off the grid." On disconnecting from our thought dominant world, they have had the opportunity to reinvigorate these unconscious skills and created a much stronger potential for *survival*. These people, more than any others, live almost solely in their *root* and *sacral centers*. They use and exhibit the evolved qualities inherent in our primordial *instincts*.

There are many of us who have learned to shut out the thoughts of the modern world. We do this by hyper-focusing on our inner urges. Eventually we become artists, musicians, sports participants, gymnasts, martial artists, dancers, tradesmen, or applicants of any other skill or capacity that allows us to detach from the world and "get lost" in the creative endeavors that resonate with our heart and our natural propensities. To wit, ask yourself when was the last time you were involved in an activity that gave you pleasure and that you totally lost track of time? This type of disconnect from the world is the most effective in aiding us in reconnecting with our basic animal *instincts*. It is in this state that we perceive the order inherent in the universe and our place in alignment with it.

Different animals have specific "dances" and rituals geared toward attracting a mate. Humans are no different except that our "dances" and rituals are also flavored with varied patterns rooted in our culturally developed traditions and social rules for personal interaction. In the same way that a peacock would spread their feathers to display attractiveness or excitement, a human may wear specific types of clothing to accentuate their bodies and interest from the opposite sex. Also, in the way a whippoorwill creates a melodious melody, or a whale produces whale song, humans produce music to engender feelings of intimacy for attracting a prospective mate. Additionally, the same way wildebeests or lions may spar with each other to exhibit their strength and prowess, a human may play sports or work out in the gym to build muscles and strength to attract a potential mate. The *sacral center* provides the venue for natural solicitation of a mate. It always seems to bleed through into social and cultural habits.

Although there are some species of animals that bond for life, most do not. Relative to humans, the same is true for humans, especially if our mate solicitation only occurs through the *sacral center*. Monogamy will be supported through higher centers.

So now, armed with an understanding of how our *instinct* works, we can now look at how imbalances in our *senses* might affect how we manifest with the *root center* and the *sacral center*. Our *senses* are the modality that resonate most clearly with how we perceive the natural order of things. We can relate to that natural order in two ways: we can either ignore or deny that we have any connection to nature, or we can immerse ourselves in it until it blinds us to the rest of life and its manifestations.

In the first case of denying our connection to nature, this may come on the heels of fearing who or what we truly are in nature and insulate us from having to acknowledge and then deal with any of our animal *instincts*. This is one of the recipes that some religions use to keep us from investing too much energy into our *senses*. This is also a pattern used by people who are fearful that their own animal nature may reveal their inadequacies in handling their *senses* while at the same time indicating that there is a requirement for them to adjust to new and integrated lifestyles. The bottom line is that they are trained to *feel* ashamed of their connection to the animal kingdom.

In the second case of immersing themselves into their *senses* to excess, their sensitivities can be used as an excuse not to be accountable for their responsibilities in ordinary daily life requirements. They will claim that it is more important to be in touch with nature than to be bothered with performing properly in social settings. It saves them from learning, and failing, to interact with others in a cordial and accommodating way. In this way, manners and culture can then be ignored. The truth is, they assert that cultural interaction is a waste of time but are really petrified of being seen as *unable* to interact successfully. In the first case, they are afraid of exposing their fear of nature. In the second, they are afraid of exposing their inability of interacting. Both approaches are equally imbalanced in integrating their *senses* into their spiritual expression.

In reference to worldly correspondences, the lowest level of the *sacral center* color would be orange. The *sacral center* also is representative of the plant kingdom with its intended evolution toward the *solar plexus center* and *feeling*. The *sacral center* also corresponds to the Seventh Ray of *Ceremonial Order* in Alice Bailey's hierarchy of esoteric and astrological ray energies. Veiled by the Moon, the planet Uranus is its closest representative. In the Kabbalah, it equates to Yesod. The glands most closely associated are the gonads and the ovaries.

THE SOLAR PLEXUS

The Moving Waves

Modes of Operation: *Generative, Feeling Based & only internally cognizant*

The *solar plexus center*, or the *Manipura* in Sanskrit, is located in a line from the notch underneath the bottom of the sternum to the middle of the back just in front of the spine. It is the center of nourishment in all senses of the word. First, it is a major food processing point and the place where we "digest" the *feelings* we've generated relative to others. It is, also, the emotional center of the body where we register our "gut feeling." In the same way we register whether we are hungry relative to our stomach being full or not, it also is where we *decide* whether our individual need for recognition by others is filled or not and why. Relative to this, it is also the seat of the *lower mind*.

As the active side of our pair of *feeling chakras (solar plexus & heart)*, the *solar plexus center* is largely concerned with *projecting* our *feelings*. This may happen *consciously* or *unconsciously*. For the majority of people, it happens *unconsciously*. Anger is probably the most projected *consciously* since when we are angry, we usually *want* people to know and *feel* that we are angry. Most of our other *feelings*, fear, affection, excitement, nervousness are usually felt only internally and are kept from others to prevent our being manipulated by them. Most of us humans are not aware that we project our *feelings involuntarily*. We most often *feel* that it is needed or proper to keep them hidden and to ourselves.

Since we don't *consciously* attach our *feelings* to the external environment, we believe that they are not noticed by others and most people don't. However, even though most people don't "notice" what we're *feeling*, they still *feel* what we *feel unconsciously* and they *involuntarily* ingest what we have projected through their *empathic* capabilities. I will cover more on this when we discuss the *heart center*.

In addition to being the seat of projected *feeling*, the *solar plexus center* is also the seat of the *lower mind*. The *lower mind* is our day to day thinking machine and deals exclusively with logic and time-based issues. It is solely grounded in tangibility. It is also our place for judgment of ourselves and others. It is the medium for our internal conversations and is also the generator of our *feelings* involved in being *possessive*. Here we *consciously* view ourselves.

Within the *lower mind* and centered in the *solar plexus center* is the matrix by which we comprehend our own existence and attempt to understand ourselves through the tangibility of the outer world. The structure of time, past, present and future, gives us the ability to separate our experiences from each other. This also reminds us that we are separate from each other. This reveals in us a *feeling* of longing to not be away from the people and things we love. These thoughts lead us to attempt to control those people and circumstances, so we don't have to live without them. Yet, due to our separateness, we can only control ourselves. Control of others and the outside world is only ephemeral at best and inevitably an impossible delusion for us to fulfill. Yet, we still try. When our consciousness is centered in the *solar plexus center*, we can't help but attempt to control the outer world.

In light of our separateness, we assess our *self-worth* in terms of how much we remain separate from who and what we love. We define our deservedness based on that separateness. Our *self-worth* is inversely proportional to our believed need for control. So, if we believe that we have little or no *self-worth*, we will tend to attempt to control people and our environment in order to prevent exposing our believed inadequacies. The more we attempt to control people and things, the lower our belief in our *self-worth*. The higher our *self-*

worth, the less we feel the *need* to control others and the environment.

Possessiveness, which is centered in the *solar plexus center*, is the act of having, holding or controlling. Its opposite is to let go, release or surrender: hence, to allow change to occur. It complements our need for security by keeping the outside world static. The need to control can be correlated to our need or believed right to *possess*. *Possessiveness* is an attempt to hold the love, positive acknowledgment and the approval of others. It is often a reaction to believed undeservedness *or* the belief that we are entitled to more than the rest of the world.

Because the *solar plexus center* is the home of our perceived *self-worth*, this also makes it the battleground for how we identify ourselves as we polarize ourselves with the world. I am. I am not. I have. I don't have. I am loved. I am not loved. I am respected and acknowledged. I am not. These are all products of our *lower mind's* judgment of our *self-worth* as a result of not only our childhood indoctrination by our parents and caretakers but our tendency to carry on those assessments and to expect their confirmation from the outside world. Our parents' approval or disapproval begins registering in our unconscious even before we become verbal. The tangibility of our *solar plexus* world anchors us in how the outer world sees us. Our perception of our *self-worth* is consequently formed as a function of our perceived approval or disapproval from both our childhood and its continuation into our adult world. When we add the *feeling* factor to the early judgments that we have made about ourselves, it becomes extremely difficult to separate, adjust or refocus those beliefs.

When we encounter the *feelings* generated by our *solar plexus center*, we must first become aware that we are having them and then work to become proficient at handling them. Since *feelings* are an inherent component of the *solar plexus center*, they become coupled with the *lower mind* tangibility of the outer world and we find ourselves simply reacting to them often without recognizing their presence or even that we generated them. The result of this coupling is what we call *emotion*. What adds to the difficulty in our recognizing *feelings* is their gradual onset.

FEELING & EMOTION: WHAT'S THE DIFFERENCE?

To begin with, *feelings* rise of their own accord. We create *emotion*. So, what exactly is an *emotion*?

The word *emotion* has its origins in the twelfth century French as *emouvoir* or to "stir up." From the Latin it is *emovere* from *ex* "out" + *movere* "to move" meaning to "move out, remove, or agitate." It was then extended to "strong *feeling*" in the 1650s and then to any *feeling* in 1808.

When we have an experience of any consequence, a *feeling* often rises within us. As we have that experience our *conscious* and *unconscious lower mind* is in full play.

During the experience we assess it as being desirable, pleasant, traumatic, avoidant, tolerable, distressing or any other *feeling* that can be attributed to our having it. It is then committed to our memory. The next time we have a similar experience, our assessing *lower mind* brings up our past judgment of it and drags along the *feeling* we have attached to it. Our *solar plexus center* then regenerates the same *feeling*. In other words, the combination of an experience and its attendant *feeling* generates a trigger which recreates the *feeling* when the *lower mind* recognizes that we are having a similar experience. Voila! We now have an *emotion*. From its etymological beginnings we can see how it can be equated with being a trigger.

So now, armed with an understanding of how our *lower mind, feelings and emotions* all interconnect, we can now look at how imbalances in our *self-worth* might manifest. There are three types or variables in its manifestation. We can have diminished *self-worth*, exaggerated *self-worth* or we can have a balanced *self-worth*. Obviously, we would want to have a balanced *self-worth*. This would show through our having a balanced concern for others, their needs and their welfare with an *equal* consideration for our own. We would neither be overindulgent nor inconsiderate of others. We would also behave the same way toward ourselves. Energy would move freely and easily between our inner world and outer world. We would basically feel at peace without any extreme urges. We would be calm and grounded and move through the world with an open mind for what the universe might present to us. When working with the *solar plexus center,* this would be our objective when working with the *solar plexus center* and what we should be striving for in terms of growing spiritual maturity.

DIMINISHED SELF-WORTH	BALANCED SELF-WORTH	EXAGURATED SELF-WORTH
Belief in Need to Control People & Circumstances	Self-Control Only	Belief in Right to Control People & Circumstances
Compensative Narcissism	Measured Humility	Overt Narcissism
Hyper-External Locus of Control	Balanced Locus of Control	Hyper-Internal Locus of Control
Hyper-Sensitivity to People & the World	Balanced Sensitivity Between the World & Self	Hypo-Sensitivity to People & the World
Inadequate Boundaries	Flexible Boundaries	Impenetrable Boundaries

Relative to our *self-worth,* there are other two manifestations, diminished and exaggerated. These are on either side of a balanced *self-worth.* They would exhibit evidence of their application when the *solar plexus center* is misaligned or utilized improperly. This would again show through how we assess and then engage our *self-worth* with the world. Our exaggerated *self-worth* is a lot less common. This is because childhoods that have been overindulged in and spoiled by their parents happen much less frequently in our western culture. The larger majority of us in the western cultures consist of having had our sense of *self-worth* diminished in our upbringing and then exacerbated in adulthood through abandoning our *self-trust* in deference to "professional" authority, receiving a total lack of encouragement from our family, friends and fellow workers and developing a progressive belief that there is an overwhelming requirement for us to have to prove ourselves and validate our actions at every juncture of personal and professional interaction. Please take a look at the *self-worth* chart.

In looking at the chart we can quickly see that our *self-worth* is based on two factors: our perspective in terms of who is in charge of our lives and the life experiences that might tend to confirm our assumptions. When the outside world is perceived in terms of being in charge of our lives, we call this having an external *locus of control*. When we believe that *we* are in control of our world, we are said to have an internal *locus of control*. Most of the world, especially those of us who have been raised to believe that tangibility is the dominant force in our lives, end up believing we have little or no control over our own lives and that other people run things. This comes from accepting that our parents make the rules and then transferring that authority to the world at large as a surrogate parent as we grow into adults. Those of us in the extreme of this and with a rebellious spirit become *compensatory narcissists* demanding that the world give us deference to our needs and wants. We tend to defend ourselves at every turn. In this case we tend to submerge our diminished *self-worth* and intentionally project an air of superiority in order to "be right" and draw that deference from others while hiding our believed unworthiness. Most *compensatory narcissists* have no idea what they are or why they feel that they must "one-up" everyone around them. In these cases, their *entitlement* is put on but *unconsciously*. Those who are aware of *feeling* diminished in *self-worth* also become *compensatory narcissists* but *know* it is so and often end up playing the victim in an attempt to make others feel sorry for them or obliged to "fix" them. The trait of helplessness is a classical symptom of having poor *self-worth*.

Those who have been indulged in and spoiled by their parents grow up believing that the world is *supposed* to over-indulge and spoil them, giving them an internal *locus of control* in the extreme. This type of upbringing tends to make them *overt narcissists* where they truly feel entitled with no *unconscious* interplay. There is no sensitivity, no remorse and often an innate ruthlessness when dealing with others. Ultimately, it is the *compensatory narcissist* who has the better opportunity for rebalancing themselves. At the core, they *know* that something is off in the way that the world responds to them because underneath, they *did* gain a modicum of sensitivity toward others in their diminished upbringing. It's a very different story for the *overt narcissist*. They haven't a clue that something is off in their interactions with others let alone that the problem originates from within.

To understand the many faces of diminished *self-worth*, I suggest reading my book *Core Values: Recognizing & Surviving the Global Assault on Our Personal Autonomy*. There I present the Seven Vices and Virtues and how they interact with our *self-worth* (2024).

It should be understood that everyone's "starting point" for growth will be different as our spirit is *drawn* into the human lineage that best provides the polarity that will lead us into our currently needed path for spiritual growth in this lifetime. If we are developing our will, we might be drawn into a family and circumstances that suppress our will. If we are to develop compassion, we might be drawn into a lifetime that causes us great pain so we may identify that pain in others. Some paths may be harder than others. Some may be easier. However, we must all go through the necessary trials and tribulations that bring forward the best parts of our spiritual expression. At the risk of sounding trite, no one escapes the law, Universal Law. It's just that we assume these paths at different times in our progression. Those who seem to have it easy may be resting and regaining their energy before they embark on their next more difficult spiritual quest. Those who are facing insurmountable odds now may be drawn to an easier lifetime in the future.

Developing a balanced sense of *self-worth* on our own is a very difficult road to hoe. Many of us take a lifetime to come to the needed realizations about ourselves telling us how we have been led to assess ourselves in an imbalanced way. This is the job for most of humanity since our point of evolving spiritual growth posits most of us in the *solar plexus center* while directing us to move toward becoming more subtle, aware and becoming grounded in the *heart center*.

The last point I need to put forward and emphasize is that the *solar plexus center* is the home of the *lower mind* and the last center where polarization will take place. It is also the last center where the concept of time will be a dominant factor in its application. Time is also a polarization in that there is *before* and *after*. It allows for the *lower mind* separation of *past* and *future* events. When we "graduate" to the *heart center*, unity becomes the perceptual sphere of its application and comprehension. *Unity cannot thrive in a polarized environment.*

In reference to worldly correspondences, the lowest level of the *solar plexus center* color would be yellow. The *solar plexus center* also is representative of the animal kingdom with its intended evolution aspiring toward the *heart center* and the "human" kingdom. The *solar plexus center* also corresponds to the Sixth Ray of *Idealism & Devotion* in Alice Bailey's hierarchy of esoteric and astrological ray energies. The planets Mars and Neptune are its closest representatives. In the Kabbalah, they equate to Hod and Netzach. The gland most closely associated is the pancreas.

THE HEART CENTER

The Quiet Space

Modes of Operation: *Receptive, Feeling Based & internally & externally cognizant*

The *heart center*, or *Anahata* in Sanskrit, lies in a line from dead center of the sternum to a point 3" below where the neck meets the shoulders in front of the spine. It embodies the process of releasing in all senses of the word. In the same way that the *solar plexus center* emphasizes a focus on acquisition and possessiveness, the *heart center* embodies the process of *letting go*. In the sense that the *heart center* listens to our *feelings* and those of others, it is also the home of our potential consciousness of *empathy*.

Because of its middle position in our lineup of *chakras* it serves as the "negotiator" between the tangible orientation of the lower three *chakras* and the energy application of the upper three *chakras*. Due to this it is imperative that it be a listening post for the inputs that the rest of the world feeds us in terms of our dynamic requirements for living our lives. In this it must be unbiased to any other view other than the smooth integration of both camps of human perspective; that is, tangibility and energy direction. In this perspective we can understand the label of *unconditional* that has been assigned to it by the people who invest in spiritual development. It must also be devoid of personal preference or what also has been provincially termed as *selfless* toward the sole benefit of others.

But the *unconditional-ness* and *selflessness* that are actually used and expressed don't necessarily measure up to the transparency and clarity that are assumed about true spiritual growth. Remembering that we are evolving from the *solar plexus center* to the *heart center*, we must understand that many of us are *not* truly focused on that transparency and clarity but are still anchored in control and possessiveness. To those *unconditional* means that the people with whom they are interacting are expected to put up no boundaries or interference to their worldly objectives that are still grounded in that control and possessiveness emanating from their *solar plexus center*. And that their *selflessness* actually contributes to them being a "non-person" who will be eminently more susceptible to their tangible world manipulation due to their modesty and lack of needing to assert themselves due to being centered in the *heart center*.

The transition from being centered in the *solar plexus center* to the *heart center* is the most difficult for our culture, especially when the whole culture is primarily centered in the *solar plexus center* and is obsessed with verifying life from an evidence-oriented perspective. Transitioning into a listening or receptive perspective when all our training has been geared toward being materially active and aggressive is like spitting into the wind in a hurricane. The mountains to be scaled are almost insurmountable. Our first requirement is to let go of the outer world's demands by pulling ourselves inside and free of the coercing forces contributing to our needing to "belong" in the tangible world and then quietly to listen to our heart. This task is like trying to hear a whisper in a room of screaming people.

In addition to the difficulty in scaling the mountain of personal purging needed to reside in the *heart center*, even New Age metaphysics has become much more mainstream and tangibly oriented. In doing so it has diluted the traditional requirements necessary to maintain spiritually consecrated studies. This includes allowing imbalances in our *solar plexus center* energies to permeate our paths of discipleship. As a result, our focus on purity has become minimized and diffused while our understanding of what is needed to advance into the *heart center* has become severely mono-focused. Those of us who are able to do this in the tsunami storm of *feelings* surrounding us become a lighthouse for others attempting to find and remain on the *heart centered* path.

Manners, encouragement and *compassionate action* are different degrees of deferred types of action permissive for a spirit to slowly take up residence in the *heart center*. They are three qualities of action that have slowly been disappearing from our western culture as our advancing material world obsession has begun to take a stronger dominance in our tangible world. The diminishing of our *self-worth* through poor childrearing has accelerated its advance. This has also diminished the *personal autonomy* of all of us to the extent that the average person has come to believe that they can have no effect on its rising tide. A sense of *hopelessness* is a primary effect of diminished *self-worth* for both parent and child. *Manners, encouragement* and *compassionate action* are powerful but gently applied antidotes toward mitigating those effects. Their use and application can gradually put us in a mindset that will incubate a *heart center* perspective while allowing us to take up partial residence in its space.

These three *heart center* dynamics, *manners, encouragement* and *compassionate action,* work under the principle of *deference.* The etymology of the word *deference* derives from the French *deferer* from the 1640s meaning to "yield in opinion, submit to the judgment of another." Other words that relate to this behavior are delay, postpone, put off, suspend, set aside, waive and allow. The question that then begs to be answered is what are we putting aside? And that would be the immediacy of our own needs and wants being answered in favor of allowing another to have, be or do *before our* personal preferences. Another way of seeing this is allowing another person precedence over our opportunity to be heard, chosen, acknowledged or consulted. This allowing is a *letting go* of our tangible world needs or wants so another may not feel pressured to have to compete or to be aggressive with us in getting or being what they want. This would gently lead them toward using *heart center* dynamics.

When our *self-worth* is balanced, this is an easy thing to do as creating an impression or covering a perceived lack or inadequacy is not what is foremost on our mind. We are relaxed, open and calm enough in our own *personal autonomy* to be able to allow another person to have over us what the tangible world would describe as an advantage. Now, let's take a look at the different degrees of *deference*.

Manners – *Manners* are specific types of "proper behavior and commendable habits of conduct" related to how we behave with others in social interactions (c. 1300). Traditionally, they are habit patterns that make relating to other people in our culture or others smoother by removing the awkwardness that often accompanies meeting people for the first time and not understanding how they might interpret our actions without perceiving difficulty. When we have and express *manners*, it "greases" our rapport with others so we may relate more easily.

Manners is one of the lesser forms of *deference*. On our part, it is passive and a lesser form in that by our having and using *manners* we simply hold ourselves back from needing to express ourselves and our opinions over others. In doing so it lowers the resistance produced in the person we are being mannered toward by diffusing some of the urgency *they* might feel in having to be competitive with us or having to defend themselves to hide their believed inadequacies. Having and using *manners* is a first step in moving toward being centered in the *heart center* rather than remaining centered in the *solar plexus center* through promoting *polarization* and possessiveness.

Encouragement – *Encouragement* is a little more of an active form of presenting *deference*. In addition to refraining from creating anything that might resemble competition, we also give support to the aspect of the rapport that we have held ourselves back on. That is, we give verbal support for what our person is trying to assert. This reduces the tension our person is feeling, and the rapport takes on a more relaxed exchange. The support we carry out aligns more with the *heart center* dynamic. This not only reduces the stress produced through any *polarization* but contributes to the energy and direction our person is trying to create and makes our *heart center* influence more dominant. *Encouragement* brings our center more into the sphere of the *heart center* by letting go of a little more of the attitude that is driven by our need for individuality and recognition. If we have a balanced or close to balanced *self-worth,* we essentially will not mind *letting go* of any minor opportunities that make us more separated or *polarized* from asserting our opinion and individuality over others.

Compassionate Action – *Compassionate action* is two steps further than *manners* and *encouragement*. Not only do we *defer* our own opinion and add a supporting voice, but we now even physically *do* something that relieves more of the stress and tension created by the competition created by low *self-worth*. In doing this we put *more* energy into minimizing the tension in the world around us. This is probably one of the highest and most beneficial types of action that we can take in the way of listening to the *heart center*. This choice usually comes as a result of our *empathizing* with the other person. That is, we also *feel* what *they* are *feeling* and it encourages the choice in us to take action either by supporting their efforts or diminishing their pain.

Each of these three actions, *manners, encouragement* and *compassionate action* are consecutively applied, each more intensely while moving us into residing more in the *heart center*. This can be done by us at any time but is more frequently done when our own *self-worth* is balanced or nearing balance. One of the goals of our spirit is to *let go* of our survival (*instincts*) and self-preserving tendencies (*solar plexus center*) enough to allow us to establish our primary residence in the *heart center*. Through our *letting go* of these tendencies sufficiently enough we can allow the *heart center* to establish that fledgling dominance without relinquishing behaviors that will maintain our personal barriers enough to keep our overall spiritual direction and integrity. This amounts to creating a very subtle shift in our energy application and conscious perspective. This balance is initially very precarious as a new residence in the *heart center* is still very susceptible to influences that will tend to pull us back into recentering in the *solar plexus center* more easily. These influences come from an *unconscious* coercion by the people we have directed our newly balanced energy toward. Since we are not yet strongly grounded in acting from the *heart center*, influences from the *solar plexus center* that are still competitive in others may drag us back into *polarizing* our own energies thereby losing our *heart center* grounding and essentially sabotaging our newly found center. Let's take a look at what we might expect to come from others.

UNCONSCIOUS SABOTEURS

When we deal with others who are still operating from the perspective of an imbalanced *self-worth*, our interaction with them pulls us back in the field of *polarization* due to their defensiveness and *feelings* of competition. For them, they still see the world as a competitive place and are fearful of having their perceived inadequacies exposed and used by others to dominate them. Under competitive pressure for *survival* and their need for recognition, their individuated ego will *unconsciously* defend itself against all perceived aggressors. This keeps them in a mindset creating and maintaining the competition that is so typical of the *solar plexus center*. What follows are some of the ploys that a threatened ego will *unconsciously* use to pull us back into competition with them.

Commiseration – With the arrival of difficulty or disappointment, most humans will seek out another person to "get it off their chest." This is an *unconscious* urge to divest themselves of the tension that they have developed from confronting a disagreeable situation. Remembering back to our discussion on energy, they're actually looking for a receptacle to take their tension so they can purge the block that's locking up their energy. This is done *unconsciously*. In answering this urge, they will seek a person who is "clear," moves their energy easily and appears to be mostly free of tension. The recipient will usually be a *heart centered* person or one who has become commonly known as a "giver." Additionally, they're also seeking mental assurance that they're not alone in their demise. When we look for someone to "share" our issues with, we are said to be seeking *commiseration*. We also know this as "misery loves company." The *heart center* person must be careful not to also get dragged into complaining or "bashing the bad guy." We can be *compassionate,* but we *don't* have to participate in reenergizing the *polarization* created by the *solar plexus center* person. This will lock *us* up in the complaining person's dilemma thereby dragging us out of our *heart centered* perspective. We can encourage that person along the lines of *letting go* but we must *never* allow ourselves to fall into complaining with them. Keeping sufficient borders is a necessity and will assist us in doing so.

Playing the Victim – When a person opts into a *victim* perspective, they are choosing to deny their accountability for their choices by applying blame for any consequences that they don't like or *feel* adequate to deal with. Placing blame puts them in a helpless perspective, giving them perceived permission to ask for or expect someone else to deal with what they don't want to. This accomplishes two things. It not only absolves them of any and all accountability for their choices, but it is also used to garner pity from family members, onlookers and "close friends." The *victim* will work hard to gain your "support" for their misfortune. The more they can make you feel sorry for them, the more you will be drawn into their ploy through pity. If you refuse to fix their problem or *commiserate* with them while relieving their "suffering" you will be accused of being selfish or lacking in *compassion.*

For the *heart centered* person with a relatively balanced *self-worth,* this is generally not a problem. We understand that most of their dilemmas are a result of the victim's own choices. The accusations of selfishness and lack of *compassion* will likely just roll off our backs.

Both the *commiserator* and the *victim* direct their energies toward *pulling us into* their mindset. In doing this they believe that we will alter our behavior and exert our efforts in their direction to "fix" their oppressive circumstances and allow them to free their tension by burdening *us* with it, thereby, freeing *their* energy and locking up *ours* in dealing with their issues. This way they gain their lost access to their own energy while shielding their perceived low *self-worth* from exposure.

Those who *project anger, induce fear* and *threaten* direct their energies toward *pushing us away* from their space. In doing this they can keep our assessment of them a mystery so we can't see or expose their imbalanced *self-worth*. This is done through *unconscious* motives. Those ploys come from the mindset of either an *overt narcissist* or a *compensative narcissist*. Remember, both of them also have imbalanced *self-worth*; the *overt* has unperceived hyper *self-worth* and the *compensative* buries their hypo *self-worth*. The *overt narcissist* doesn't know that they have a hyper *self-worth* and pushes us away out of arrogance and superiority. The *compensative narcissist* might have known at an earlier time but now submerges their awareness of their hypo *self-worth* into their *unconscious* and pushes us away out of *self-convinced* entitlement.

Projecting Anger – When a person opts to *project anger,* they are confronted with being accountable for the disagreeable consequences of their choices. They truly believe that they should not be held liable for the choices that they have made unless it shows their image as socially positive. They *project anger* because they are feeling insulted that they must defend themselves but *unconsciously* are fearful of being exposed as being incompetent or inadequate. The *anger* serves as a smoke screen while they push away those who might expect something from them that they consider undesirably revealing. The fear is only in the *unconscious* of the low *self-worth person*. The *overt narcissist* feels no fear. Their *conscious* feeling one of is indignation. In current day perspectives, both the *overt narcissist* and the *compensative narcissist* will act "offended." For many people this has become a tool to use in social interactions that might reveal their imbalanced *self-worth*. It serves as a distraction and avoidance technique used against being held accountable or honestly assessing themselves.

For the *heart centered* person with a long standing and relatively balanced *self-worth,* this is generally not a problem unless that balanced *self-worth* is shaky or new. Generally, we can just let the *projector* rant and rave and let their discharge roll off our backs. For those of us who have had bad experiences dealing with people's *anger,* we might find ourselves thrown off balance for a bit. However, most of us who have a balanced *self-worth* will come to ignore the ranters and not take it personally after thinking about where their anger might actually be coming from. For new *heart center* dwellers, it may drive us back into the *fear* aspect of the *solar plexus center* for a while until we re-establish our commonsense grounding.

Threatening or ***Creating Fear*** – When a person opts to *threaten,* they also desire to avoid being accountable for the disagreeable consequences of their choices. But they themselves are hesitant to *project anger* as they are also fearful of being confronted by anger themselves. Using a ploy to trigger an unpredictable *emotional* response in another is too big a risk to take as they might not know how to handle receiving anger themselves. Rather they will choose to use *mental* coercion to create a possible future state in others by warning of disagreeable circumstances. To *threaten* circumstances about what *might* happen in another would appear to be safer than using *emotion* to actually create them. The possible verbiage might go, "If you don't leave me alone, you'll be sorry for what comes back to you." This is designed to not only push others away but to also make them fearful of what *might* occur. The hope and intention is that their believed inadequacy might not be discovered.

EMPATHY

Empathy is when you simultaneously *feel* what another person is *feeling*. It is NOT *sympathy. Sympathy* is a *mental* consideration where you'd say I *understand* how you *feel* and it may evoke a *feeling* but often isn't included in our reactions.

Empathy can occur either *consciously* or *unconsciously,* however, *it will be felt involuntarily.* Essentially, we are receivers that are tuned to everyone's *feelings.* Because we are receivers, *feeling* will be automatically received and processed. As it is processed it is passed through our *solar plexus center.* We may or may not recognize it as it is happening. However, *feelings* will register in our body, whether we are *conscious* of them or not. Our body also reacts to them, again, whether we recognize them or not. We all pick up the *feelings* of those who are close or intimate with us and we simply react to them not realizing they came from someone else. Even if we recognize *what* we are *feeling,* we just assume that they are of our own making.

The main task for all of us is to first, recognize that we are picking up what others are *projecting* and then give ourselves permission to just let it pass without holding on to what we're *feeling* coming from them. The moment we take hold, our body reacts. It's very much like eating something that is bad. If we spit it out, there is usually no problem. But if we swallow it, we will have to deal with its effects.

When we are with other people most of us don't realize that we are constantly "ingesting" their projection, especially if we are close or intimate with them. It most commonly happens with families and spousal relationships. This is so because when we are with them, we are tuned to and open to them. Those in our family *unconsciously* also "have our buttons" so they *intuitively* know what we will most likely respond to and how. This is one of the reasons why it is the hardest to change ourselves when we deal with our family. It is their lineage or wavelength that has programmed us for our life lessons, so it is something that resonates with us to our core.

This leaves it to us to first, recognize we are picking it up and second, take steps to not allow it to stay in our focus. The easiest way to disconnect from coursing it through our bodies internally is to not give it mental momentum by focusing on the *feeling*. One of the easiest ways is to follow Buddhist meditation recommendations telling us to simply allow the *feeling* to wash over us without putting our attention into it. For most people, this is easier said than done. When most of us have a *feeling* and recognize it, regardless of good or bad, we have the tendency to focus on it or even obsess over it. This has the effect of intensifying the force of our reaction to it. When we *don't* recognize it, we simply react and its influential effects are slightly less. But *our need is to recognize it* and short circuit its effects by either allowing it to wash over us without our mental participation or to change the channel. By "change the channel," we mean simply changing our attention to something else thereby not giving it any extra energy or momentum. This keeps its effects to a minimum and allows it to ebb away through natural attrition that normally builds and ebbs like a wave. Remember, *feelings* are not controllable and come *without* our initiative. They ebb and flow in their own way and time. We simply have to wait for them to diminish of their own accord. We can simply say, "and this too shall pass."

In coming to reside in the *heart center* our primary task is to be able to use the *solar plexus center's* energies but not to become trapped in them by promoting and sustaining a tangible world and polarized mindset. At the root of this, establishing a balanced *self-worth* is essential. This must be accomplished if we are to be able to reside in the *heart center* to any great extent. Since we are human and knowing that to be dwelling in the *heart center* is the objective of our current incarnation's evolutionary intent, we all must work to bring our awareness of our *feelings* to the surface of our consciousness. This is much more difficult than we might anticipate.

Knowing the state of our *self-worth* is a challenge at best since we know that some of the mechanisms that maintain a *polarized* disposition operate *unconsciously* through the *solar plexus center* and are very easily triggered by others. Studying ourselves and our reactions to what we *feel* should therefore be the centerpoint of our efforts. The beginning efforts of this is often putting ourselves in a *quiet space* and replaying our experiences with and reactions to our interactions with the world. Since most of our lives have become faster paced and more intense, this in itself is a challenge. But for us to gain residence in the *heart center* it is an absolute necessity.

Many spiritual disciplines have practices that can establish and then enhance that *quiet space* with many recommendations on how to proceed in order to gain the most benefit from the practice. But again, the mainstream media has diluted many of these practices by commercializing them into a form that simplifies the action so much that the depth and intensity of what is needed is lost. The best way of ensuring that the thoroughness of what we need to do originates from translated scriptures in concert with a traditional teacher. Even then some of the translated scriptures may omit some of the most important features needed for our attention. Please note that I didn't say a "qualified" teacher. In these times there are many who have skimmed the practices and created a "program" that is supposed to elicit the clarity we seek from a "one size fits all" perspective while coming from an "acclaimed qualified" instructor. In the same way that a psychotherapist may persistently bring up complexes intensifying their energy, these ill-performed practices can often do more harm than good.

The primary currency of the *heart center chakra* is *empathy*. Our *empathy* can only be recognized by listening inside. It is this *quiet-space* that is necessary to be able to do this with any sense of subtlety or accuracy. The more we do this, the more easily we will recognize when we are *empathizing*. The overall objective is to be able to do this at the moment that it is happening. Recognizing it when it is happening will allow us to counteract any reactions that normally occur *unconsciously* before they intensify and transmit through our bodies.

In our evolution from the *solar plexus center* to the *heart center* there are many levels of awareness evident in the public. The most obtuse of these is the native who has no belief that anyone radiates *feelings* let alone picks them up and discriminates them. The *most* aware of these will be *very* few in number, undetectable by us or anyone else and probably well aware beyond what we may be working with. People of this caliber of development never divulge themselves either because of humbleness and/or a preference to not to be harmed or to have to defend themselves.

It is here in the *heart center* that we must actively choose to follow the *middle path* between the *path of mercy* and the *path of severity* as described in the teachings of the Kabbalah. Simply put, the *path of severity* is where we attempt to *force* the outer world to abide by our personal preferences that reinforce our mental resistance limiting the conditions that ensure the preservation and immovability of our security against having to allow change in our consciousness. Its extreme brings pain and disappointment through the world's resistance to our attempted assertions. The *path of mercy* is where we completely *allow* the world to be and have what *it* wants to have *sacrificing* our personal values and preferences so as not to face or be accountable for the action we must take in order to open our consciousness to the growth required to follow the *middle path*. Its extreme brings regret and hopelessness. The Western World has most often followed the *path of severity* attempting to control life's conditions in order to create an immoveable *feeling* of security. The Eastern World has most often followed the *path of mercy* in order to escape the tangible world's imposed conditions of insecurity, hence, their belief in an acceptance of their "fate."

The *middle path* requires us to sometimes allow *deference* and sometimes to take *action*. The discrimination of which to do when is the most poignant challenge facing our residence in the *heart center*. Our effort to do so must remain perseverant and diligent. Let's look at the two opposing paths, *severity* and *mercy*, and see how they might manifest in our life circumstances if we were to follow one extreme or the other.

In looking at the two mindsets, I will describe them in the extreme for us to make no mistake about the behaviors that might erupt from either of them. Please keep in mind that depending on the circumstances that we are faced with, these behaviors might erupt selectively and with differing directions and intensity with each person. Both sets of behavior, especially in the extreme, emanate from the home of *polarizing*, that is, the *solar plexus center*, from which we are working diligently to evolve "above." Many of us may exhibit mild symptoms of both, but in indifferent situations. However, regardless of the intensity level and as a general rule, we will usually gravitate toward one side more than the other. With that being said, let's proceed with explaining the dynamics.

THE PATH OF SEVERITY MINDSET

This seems to be one of the more common directions our thinking might take when pursuing life's activities and requirements, especially, in our Western Culture. When we are embedded in this type of thinking, we find that the world just doesn't fit in the ways we believe that the world *should* behave and react. We hold beliefs and assumptions that there is a "right way and wrong way" that should be followed by everyone. Our belief on how things *should* be for us becomes a template for how we expect the world *should* treat us. It is this assumption that becomes the possessive and controlling aspect of the *solar plexus center* that traps us in the *path of severity*. We feel that we must always *do* something. Letting the world act on its own is seen almost as a sense of laziness. To us it feels as if the world constantly needs to be fixed and adjusted by us in ways that match our assumptions on how things should be. We feel frustrated but also *feel* and assume that others are either inadequate to the tasks at hand or that they personally disrespect us because they either don't act on or understand life in ways that we believe are right, proper, or appropriate for how life *should* be lived. We then feel that we must direct and guide them. In this way we often attempt to monitor or manage others while honestly believing that we know best and that only *we* "know" is what is appropriate for them.

Our actions are done in a spirit of "this is for your own good" or "I'm only trying to help." We might also use assumed generalizations stating that "this is the way *everyone* else does it" or "*everyone* knows this" while attempting to coerce others into performing along *our* assume path of "appropriate" action. This type of thinking also makes us feel exempt from being held accountable for "making the rules." When others insist on doing things their own way or refuse to follow our "recommended' advice, we become angry and upset with them because we honestly can't understand why they won't do things in a way that is, to us, obviously in their own best interest and, of course, the "right" way.

This perspective emanates from a low *self-worth* perspective and an internal *locus of control*. Our attempt to control the world arises from a need to force the rest of the world into a mode of action that offers respect to us and our preferences not realizing that this attempted coercion is simply a compensation to eclipse our own perceived inadequacies in handling life as it is presented to us. If we can get others to do things in our own preferred way, our perceived inadequacies will remain hidden from public view and our socially created image will remain intact. Our "security" will then be assured. The more ardently we attempt to control the world, the more deleterious and thoroughly undermining our *self-worth* issues have become. In the extreme we will find bullies and intimidators emanating from this perspective. Relative to Sigmund Freud's psychosexual stages of development, *anal retentive* best exemplifies this imbalance.

CONSEQUENCES OF THE PATH OF SEVERITY

The more resistance we produce against allowing the world to be and present itself to us as it is, the stronger the consequences of our immovability will be. It takes a tremendous amount of energy to resist the flow of the world. It locks up even more of our energy when we attempt to prevent our perceived inadequacies from being discovered. The pressure this creates on our bodies can be lethal. To begin with, this tends to raise our blood pressure, so we may seem and act like a type "A" personality. But more importantly, the diseases that result from this kind of perpetual effort are dangerous and ultimately lead to some very dire consequences. With other contributing factors such as poor diet, it can also lead to heart failure.

One of the shorter-term effects is to develop an ulcer. Ulcers come from persistent stress in attempting to overcome or prevent outside influences from affecting our choices and preferences in how we conduct our lives. Ulcers occur within the sphere of the *solar plexus center*. These develop as a result of our obsessive tendency toward our attempted control of the tangible world, hence, their physical manifestation. They are generally reversable, however, most of us who maintain a perspective aligned with the *path of severity* rarely adjust our perspective enough to make a difference in our consequences. The danger of life-coping consequences also occurs after long-term persistence. These most commonly occur in the form of dementia and Alzheimer's. Let's take a look at the dynamic.

When we are younger, we have a high amount of energy to pursue life and its requirements. We tend to take on many tasks and projects often to the limits of our ability to utilize our energy whether efficiently or not. As we get older and as our body starts to lose some of its endurance and flexibility, our energy reserve is taxed more heavily for its recovery and maintenance while we still attempt to maintain the intensity and persistence of our activities. If we are at all obsessive, and this is true of many *path of severity* natives; we continue our pace and our intensity well past our energy's capacity to accommodate all that we feel must be controlled. As our energy gets more locked up in our fixations, less is available to maintain and recover our aging physical body. Access to our energy is now no longer as available as it was when we were younger. When we just "can't let things go," what we did have control over previously now begins to fall apart due to the lack of available energy. As these continued tasks overwhelm us and our body continues to age, our memory, mental capacity and acuity also suffer more energy loss. We slowly devolve into a cascade of physical and perceptual operational failures. Symptoms of dementia and Alzheimer's begin to show themselves. However, if these ailments *aren't* present and we *are* able to *mentally* stay fixated, then our heart may become the victim resulting in an equally catastrophic failure. Regardless of our intent, as we age, we no longer have access to energy to maintain control of our fixated circumstances or our bodies.

DEALING WITH THOSE ON THE PATH OF SEVERITY

Arguing with those locked in the *path of severity* doesn't work. We need the courage and the strength to present *deference*. This lets them do what they wish but doesn't present a commitment from us aligning with their perspective. Their need to "be right" is often indefatigable. For those of us who focus on maintaining that our directives come from the *heart center*, it is imperative that we first hold to our boundaries. This will initially prevent us from being coerced into acquiescing to the control needs of the native on the *path of severity*. They will do all they can do to convince us that we are wrong in our approach to how we are handling the current situation or even our own lives. Moving us into aligning with their perspective is their prime directive. They believe that if they can do that, they will feel that their believed and hidden inadequacies are safe from exposure. If we align with them acquiescing to their perspective, we simply aid and abed their self-deception.

Our response should be along the lines of "I understand how you feel" and then proceed to do what *we* feel is best for our growth and that of the *path of severity* native. We *don't* need to explain ourselves, although those on this path may insist that we do so. Those who hold more aggressively to this path will often insistently interrogate us as to *why* with the intention of picking apart our reasoning from a logical tangible world perspective. But the *heart center* is not founded on tangible worldly logic. Our center comes from a different space. If we can simply say that it just doesn't *feel* right, they will have little or no ability to convince us otherwise. The logic of their *lower mind* is essentially incapable of dealing with our *feelings*. Remember, they are still operating from the *solar plexus center* where they have yet to understand and deal with their own *feelings* from a balanced perspective let alone understand or accept ours. Most operating from this center still have their *feelings* buried, ignored or subject to their *lower mind's* discrimination.

Deference doesn't mean giving in. Although, to those on the *path of severity* they may see it as such. Our enemies in this interaction are our pride and our need to be loved and accepted. The logic of the native locked in the *path of severity* is to make us feel a diminished sense of *self-worth* or even shame if we refuse to align with their perspective. If we don't, we likely may receive disparagement accusing us of cowardice, prejudice, lack of compassion, selfishness, or any other host of defamatory accusations designed to diminish our *self-worth* in their perception of our social standing.

THE PATH OF MERCY MINDSET

As much as the *path of severity* aligns with the need for control, the *path of mercy* is primarily averse toward any kind of control, by self or others. Whether *conscious* or *unconscious*, the immature version of this mindset emanates from an avoidance of accountability for any action that *might* be expected of us or need to be taken. The appearance of this perceived irresponsibility shows itself though our reluctance to deal with our issues directly. We essentially do this *unconsciously* attempting to avoid any action that might expose our potential inability to behave or act in a competent way. Remember, those on the extreme *path of mercy* also have compromised *self-worth* but handle it in a way opposite to those on the *path of severity*. Rather than confront it, we avoid it. For us, out of sight is out of mind. To distract from our avoidance, we have many self-deceiving defenses that will disconnect us from being accountable. Let's take a look at a few rationalizations used to prevent having to act immediately or directly.

Conserving energy - Self-preservation reasoning simply puts off the necessity to act in any immediate fashion thereby preventing performance that might risk personal failure.

Non-interference – One of the rationalizations against risking failure or embarrassment, especially if there are others who need or are owed something by us, is to claim that we don't want to deprive them of learning their lessons themselves without being rescued. We don't want to deprive someone of their autonomy. Another version of this is *letting nature take its course.*

Passive aggressive – This excuse uses messing up a small issue dissuading others from expecting us to take any effective action. This eliminates the potential for our major embarrassments thereby preventing a much larger exposure of our believed incompetence.

Making oneself scarce – We simply disappear when it becomes apparent that we will have to take some kind of action that might expose our believed incompetence.

Not My Job – Simply refusing to do something that others may claim is our responsibility.

Let Go and Let God – In "letting go" there is a word of caution needed. This quality can also be used as a vehicle for escaping or avoiding our responsibility for ourselves. We may let go of much more than what is appropriate for remaining a "responsible" adult. Those of us who espouse to "let go and let God" may be shirking accountability for the difficulties that we created. In this light, absolution can certainly be viewed by some as a convenient escape.

Procrastination – This is probably one of the most common responses as it is the most effective at avoiding being accountable. The premise is that if we are never "finished" with what needs to be addressed, we can never be held accountable for it under the guise of "not being done yet." Essentially, in barely beginning to address what needs to be done our rationalization says since we aren't actually avoiding it, we can't be held accountable for it. This is also one of the most self-deceptive tactics we can employ. Underlying the avoidance, whether conscious or not, is the fear of either having to deal with criticism of our work or punishment for an inadequate job. Although the completion of a job sometimes *is* dependent on timing, this is almost never a factor on the radar of a habitual *procrastinator*.

When we are allowed in our childhood to slip into these kinds of irresponsible thinking, we learn to feel that it is not necessary for us to fit into the way the world believes that *we* should behave and react. We develop the beliefs and assumptions that everyone has their own path to follow, hence, *we* shouldn't be interfered with. With this belief becomes the template for us to be expecting that the world *should* leave us to our own devices. It is this assumption that becomes the "free of restrictions" aspect of the *solar plexus center* that traps us in the extreme of the *path of mercy*. It is intensely rebellious, and we often become indignant when the world's attempts to coerce us into following *their* way of thinking. We come to espouse that it isn't always necessary to *do* something. To us, letting the world act of its own accord is seen almost as a sense of being fated. To us it feels as if the human world is constantly meddling and needing to fix and adjust *us* in ways that interfere with how things should naturally progress. While feeling frustrated with others, we also come to believe and assume that *they* are inadequate and/or neurotic in their understanding of the world, which should be free of human influence while having its own natural way of operating. It is for this reason that we believe that *they* interfere with and disrespect our privacy because we either don't act on or understand life in ways that *they* believe are right, proper, or appropriate for us. We assume that they *feel* that they have the right to direct and guide us. We *feel* that they too often attempt to monitor or manage us while honestly believing that they know best and that only *they* "know" what is appropriate for us. We hear that their actions are mostly done in a spirit of "this is for your own good" or "I'm only trying to help." We also encounter generalizations from the world stating that "this is the way *everyone* else does it" or "*everyone* knows this." We don't buy into it.

The *path of mercy* has been one of the less common directions taken by Westerners. We've found it mostly in the Eastern Cultures. However, they have found the *path of severity* as puzzling to them as we have found their adopted *path of mercy* to us. Historically, this has been a primary distinction between the Eastern and Western hemispheres. But as Westerners become more familiar and utilize more Eastern philosophies and perspectives and Easterners become more Westernized, this distinction seems to be fading.

Being totally *unconditional* is a fantasy and a functional assumption of those who are evasive of responsibility on the extreme *path of mercy*. It is what is also suggested by our mainstream media and spun as a being a "necessary" characteristic on the road toward popular spiritual growth. In some circumstances *unconditionalness is* necessary in order to overcome some of the obsessive materialism imposed by our physical world. But as a "cure all" band aid to the problems the Western World faces in its pursuit of spiritual wisdom, it falls sadly short of the conscious awareness that is needed to move toward the *middle path.* In this way it becomes just another excuse posed by those of us on the extreme *path of mercy,* alleviating us of any accountability or responsibility for life's simple necessities.

CONSEQUENCES OF THE PATH OF MERCY

When we evade the applying of energy to any of the normal tasks of daily living, our overall welfare suffers. We may not initially see it but when eventually what we don't do that needs to be done catches up with us, we find ourselves in an even more diminished state of *self-worth* that must further be hidden and defended. To our chagrin, this compounds our accountability problem. At the time of our required response, we usually feel that freedom from scrutiny is much more important. However, when the chickens come home to roost, we feel cornered and angry and usually blame those who draw our attention to our neglect. The more excuses we make, the more contradictions we become subject to. Then our self-image suffers all the more greatly without us ever understanding how we arrived at such a debacle.

Most of us who follow an extreme *path of mercy* never come to understand the simplicity of what can be done to avoid our feeling cornered and too often focus on those around us whom we believe are demanding the responsibility from us never realizing that the faux pas was a result of our own choices. The polarity of the "nag" and the victim mentality invariably becomes the theme of the extremist on the *path of mercy*. Ultimately, administering *tough love* becomes one of the only solutions for correcting our lack of awareness.

DEALING WITH THOSE ON THE PATH OF MERCY

Pressing the issue of accountability with us on the extreme *path of mercy* only breeds resistance and indignance due to our lack of self-awareness. The simple solution is to predict the outcome of our neglect, inform us and then simply walk away without getting involved in defending your observations. Our argument is used only to pick apart your reasoning to prove ourselves valid in our avoidance of what we are being held responsible for. Developing self-awareness can be our only solution.

RECOVING FROM EITHER EXTREME

For those of us on the extreme of either path, *severity* or *mercy*, comprehending the lesson that we must learn must break through our mindset of either coercion or avoidance. It is probably faster for those of us upon the extreme *path of severity* to realize our difficulty because our attempted coercion maintains a focus on what we want to happen. Therefore, awareness of the problem remains close at hand. Yet, we must still come to the realization that our own persistence is the difficulty that we must personally overcome in order to return to the *middle path.*

Those of us on the extreme *path of mercy* will usually take a bit longer. Since our tactic is to avoid the difficulty of accepting accountability, we continue to strive to push it out of our mind thereby pushing our becoming aware of our problem further afield. It is only when we see the eventual consequences of our neglect that we might comprehend that it is only our own ignorance in maintaining our refusal to be responsible that has kept us from moving on to the *middle path.*

SUMMARY OF HANDLING THE PATHS

I have spoken primarily of the paths from an extreme perspective in order to easily show distinct and recognizable behaviors that sustain each of their dynamics. The most important thought to put forward in this summary is that our participation in either set of dynamics can vary tremendously in concentration and the intensity with which we invest our energies in them. Some of us may be far to the right or left of the *middle path* and some of us may exhibit only mild symptoms or indications of following either path. As a general rule, most of us operate closely to the *middle path* since we are attempting to stay close to what is needed to be centered in our *heart center*. The milder the indications, the closer we are to working on the *middle path*. The more intense the indications, the further we are from working on the *middle path*.

If we were to look at these two paths from a psychosexual perspective, the extreme *path of severity* would be equivalent to Freud's categorization of being an *anal rententive* character and would typically be compulsive, neat, precise and passive aggressive. The extreme *path of mercy* would be equivalent to Freud's *anal expulsive* character which would be personally messy, reckless and defiant.

BOUNDARIES

In dealing with *heart center* dynamics there are two steps which must be followed that will allow us to solidify our centering on the *middle path*. First, we must become *unconditional* about what we let into our *consciousness*. This means that all or our motives for our ego preservation, *conscious* and *unconscious*, must become known. Once that is accomplished, we must discriminate the basis for each of our intentional limitations and separate out the ones that support the *lower mind* security, let them pass and preserve the *boundaries* for the motives that might actually support our spiritual integrity and allow the energy clear passage toward our *throat center* for actualization.

Simply put, we must ditch everything that supports the coverup of our low *self-worth* and feed the *throat center* the ability to use *boundaries* that would best maintain our spiritual integrity and foster and protect our individual lessons and those of others. It is only when we have accomplished this that we will have aligned our *heart center* with the human evolution required to raise the *kundalini* along its path without deleterious effects.

The low *self-worth* that occupies the *lower mind* essentially comes from either being anchored in the *path of severity* or the *path of mercy*. The defense mechanisms that produce their coverups of our believed inadequacies must be eliminated. This can only come from our awareness, confrontation, acknowledgment and then releasing of them. Only then can we have a clear field to approach the *middle path*. Even a mild anchor in either of the paths can have a disturbing effect on our balance.

Our insecurities can only exist as *polarized* perspectives projected in the *solar plexus center*. In the *heart center* there are no *polarized* perspectives. By the time we have centered ourselves on the *middle path,* all that has defined our separateness from others due to our insecurities has been eliminated. However, we can *utilize* those *polarizations* freely to assist others in finding their way toward the *middle path* but due to our own purging we should no longer have any emotional investment in them.

Here I would like to remind you again that the *solar plexus center* is the home of the *lower mind* and the last center where *polarization* can take place. It is also the last center where the concept of time will be a dominant factor in its application. Remember too that time is also a *polarization* of *before* and *after*. Its use confirms that there is still a presence of the operating *lower mind* through its separation of *past* and *future* events. When we "graduate" to the *heart center, unity* becomes the perceptual sphere of its application and comprehension. Here, there is no room for *polarization* of any kind. This understanding is what is behind the process of establishing *unconditionalness* or the absence of conflicting contributors. Conditions are part of a *polarized* environment. *Unity cannot thrive in a polarized environment.* The *heart center* presents us with *unity* and *unconditionalness* and sets the proper environment for the use of our *intuition* as used by the *throat center*. An explanation of this will follow in the *throat center* section shortly.

Remember, the *solar plexus center* is a generator of *feeling* and the *heart center* is simply a listening center that allows us to discriminate our *feelings* and those of others. The most important thing to comprehend here is that *empathy makes us aware of what we are still triggered by* as produced by our *lower mind* and our *solar plexus center*. It taps into our *emotional* patterns and lets us know what it is that we still have to purge in order to become clear-hearted.

In reference to worldly correspondences, the lowest level of the *heart center* color would be green, dark green for older growth and light green for newer. The *heart center* also is representative of the human kingdom with its intended evolution aspiring toward the *throat center*. The *heart center* also corresponds to the Second Ray of *Love & Wisdom* in Alice Bailey's hierarchy of esoteric and astrological ray energies. The planets Jupiter and Sun are its closest representatives. In the Kabbalah, they equate to Tiphareth. The gland most closely associated is the thymus.

THE THROAT CENTER

The Lightning Bolt

Modes of Operation: *Generative, Intuitively Based & internally cognizant only*

The *throat center*, or Vishuddha in Sanskrit, lies in a line between a spot just above the larynx and back from the chin to the hollow in the base of the skull. This center is generally referred to as the center of *will*. This is the place on the throat where we develop a "lump" when we have something to assert but have difficulty saying it. This is a contemporary connection to our aspect of personal *will*. One of the earliest uses of the word *will* comes from the fourth century B.C. Sanskrit *vrnoti* and Gothic *waljan* meaning to choose or prefer. Essentially, the word is taken to mean the implication of *intention* or *volition*. I call this center the *Lightning Bolt* because its function imparts it with the capacity to create unity through neutralizing *polarity*.

This is the first energy center presenting an ability to deal with and perceive life from an abstract perspective. This might be considered the "lower edges" of the *higher mind*. The word abstract comes from the 14th century Latin word *abstractus* "drawn away." It was also described as "withdrawn or separated from material objects or practical matters." Since the *lower mind* gains its strength and perspective from the *solar plexus center* comprised of details, specifics and facts, we may assume that an *abstract* perspective is reflective of the *higher mind* and might be more conceptual, interrelated, organizational and implied. It therefore participates in the world from a different perspective than the three "lower" centers below the heart. Additionally, the action that takes place is much more subtle and internal. This is not to be confused with the idea of *locus of control*. It has less to do with tangible motivation than it does with generating and receiving information from sources other than the physical world. As the "lower" centers are much more *instinctive* and *feeling* oriented, the "higher" centers operate more through *intuition*.

The words *instinct, feelings* and *intuition* have been used interchangeably by the majority of the world's population. The subtle difference in their meanings has escaped detection largely due to the fact that the commonly agreed upon validation of information we receive about our physical world must be based on physical clues, logic and rationalities, vis a' vis; evidence (from Latin *ex-* "out of, from" and *videre* "to see"). Validation of *intuition* is considered *irrational feeling* and is not acceptable except where there is a belief that there is a rational explanation but that we are just unable to "see" it at the moment. How far we will allow this point to be stretched, I believe, is just a matter of what personal reality is based on for each of us. If we belong to a scientific group, there is almost no "wiggle" room. If we belong to a religious group, almost anything connected to "faith" is acceptable. Essentially, it all boils down to our individual experience and the groups we choose to share our values with. However, this is not the difference I wish to clarify. The origins of the words give us clues to their "true" meanings. We have covered *instinct* and *feeling* at length in other sections. Now, let's take a look at *intuition*, the *conduit* and *modality* of the *throat center* and the *Ajna* or *third eye center*.

The word *intuition* comes from the 15th century Latin word *intueri* meaning "look at, consider" from *in-* "at, on" + *tueri* "to look at, watch over." The derivative 14th century Latin word *tutorem* adds the meaning of "guardian, watcher." Through these meanings we can see that the word *intuition* does *not* simply imply performing an *observable* action. However, observing, becoming aware and will projections *are all actions in themselves* and just not something that is usually apparent to others unless they are verbalized. *These* are the actions that are correlated with the *throat center*.

Here the action is a matter of choice *not a reaction* as it would be to that of either *instinct* or *feeling* which both operate in *polarized* fields. The action of the *throat center* creates a projection that ultimately leads to a *manifestation*. It is proactive and a function of *will*.

In the *Landscape* section, please take another look at the *Innate Modes of Perception*. Notice that *intuition* is a *conduit* used by both the *throat center* and the *third eye center*. However, in the *throat center* it is generative and becomes a *manifestation*. In the *third eye center* it is receptive and used to create awareness.

For our purposes, *intuition* is simply a *conduit* used in the *throat center* and the *third eye*. By itself, it is NOT a creation but simply the medium used. In other words, as in music, *intuition* can be thought of as *vibration* but is not the created music. It is the *vibration* that is used to *transport* music. Music is the *manifestation*. In radio, *vibration* is the carrier wave, but the music is the carried *manifestation*. In the Pony Express, the horse and rider are the *vibration* but the mail is the transported *manifestation*.

When we project what we want or need in the tangible world from the *solar plexus center*, it is a *very* different process from when we do so from the *throat center*. The *solar plexus center* is based on operating between *polarized* perspectives. These include the *path of severity* vs. the *path of mercy*, the time dimensions of before vs. after and many other details, which also sometimes conflict. These are all negotiated by the *lower mind* which is the principal agent of the *solar plexus center*.

When we project from the *throat center*, it's a whole different ball game. It is the second *chakra* past the *solar plexus center*. Everything from the *heart center* and above operates in a different dimension free of *polarities* so the medium of transmission will be different. Once we arrive at the *heart center, polarized* content is no longer present. Everything is perceived through an eye of unity. There are no opposites. There is no time and nothing to cause any perceived separation of contributing factors. Our *intuition* operates as a *Gestalt*. This is one of the reasons that our *lower mind* has such difficulty in elucidating dreams. It's all happening *at the same time* and when the *lower mind* attempts to discriminate it in a linear fashion, it's lost in translation. *Intuition* bears a striking resemblance to our dream state. In this way, the *throat center* is also the home of the *abstract*.

The projection of the *throat center* can be perceived as an act of *will*. It is a unified projection. It is the projection of a completed "picture." Projecting a *manifestation* is a willful act and the projection of a completely formulated wish. That is, there is no time, there are no discriminating factors, there is only a complete and projected integration of what we *project*. Before and after are integrated as happening in the eternal now. All parts are aligned, connected and in harmony. It occurs in a flash like lightning. We perceive and project it in its finished form as already completed. It becomes a living "thought form" through the infusion of our spirit.

One of the most difficult things for us to comprehend, especially if our primary basis for reality is our *lower mind*, is the comprehension of timelessness. The *lower mind* separates everything into before and after and into what separates our experiences from each other. Its security exists in putting everything into a linear progression that can be understood from the tangible perspective of before and after. To lose this sense of separation is terrifying to earthly grounded humans but within the natural perception of our spirit. To lose this distinction puts us at the edge of *The Abyss* in the *Tree of Life*.

TANGIBLE AVENUES OF EFFECT

The *throat center* has long been a point of energetic influence through physical contact. Other than through physical assault, the majority of the population has been un*conscious* of this potential. Yet, there has been a plethora of actions that have taken place between us that have gone virtually unrecognized.

If we're at all metaphysically observant, we likely believe that at the least energy can be transmitted or absorbed through touch by virtue of contact with another person. The touch part is right. But we must also remember that the energy we have at our disposal is constant and is subject to how much of it is tied up in the tension that we saddle the *lower mind* with. When it feels like we've gained energy, we have simply vented the tension holding it hostage. We can do this through different kinds of activities, or we can do this through another person. When we do it with another person, they either have assisted in providing an avenue for us to vent it ourselves or *they* have become our discharge point and the receptacle for it. Let's examine a few examples of how this might occur.

One of the first and simplest examples is when we feel bad, are down or are in pain one of the things we yearn for is a hug from a loving or considerate person. This in itself allows for the discharge of our tension into the person we're hugging. It may also not progress as a discharge into them from *their* perspective because they know that they have no emotional tendency to hold on to things and are able to just let it go once contact has been made. The motivation of the person providing the hug speaks volumes about how the tension will be handled. If their *self-worth* is low and they are emotionally compensative, it is likely that they will absorb the tension and need to find another outlet for it themselves. If their *self-worth* is fairly balanced, they will be able to let it go easily since they have trained themselves to not let the outside world coerce their decisions about themselves.

It's also important to note that there is an easy path from our *throat center*, "housing" our personal *will,* directly down through our arms and out through the palms of our hands. This is one of the quickest and easiest channels for tension and energy movement. The other paths move down the trunk of the body, through the legs and out through an exit point in the forward part of the arch. We can *consciously* ground out any tension we have picked up by passing it through either the hands or feet into the ground through these points or by placing our hands under running water. Healers utilize these methods to clear themselves before they move on to their next client. As per the principles ruling the *throat center*, we need to see this as complete while doing it.

In another example I must use a setup to provide an avenue for the understanding of physics. We have all shuffled our feet across a shag rug only to shock ourselves with the static electricity when we touch a metal object. The friction we create by dragging our feet builds a charge in our bodies. When we touch the metal object and since the metal is not charged, there is a difference in static charge between the two of us. The metal becomes the place that will easily neutralize the charge. We feel this as the shock when the exchange takes place. The same thing happens with people even though the rug may not be present or necessary to create the charge. People create their own tension and need a place to discharge. Hence, they become those "touchy" people that most of us avoid. We've all had that skeevy feeling when someone attempts to put their hands on us and we just *know* the it's not going to feel good or right. So, we move or squirm to avoid their touch. These people don't know that they are trying to discharge their tension. All they know is that they always feel better after they have touched someone.

Beyond simply discharging, some people use touch to coerce. That is, if we're in an exchange with them in which we either don't see something their way, we don't want to align with their perspective, or we're simply not paying attention to them, they will touch us during the conversation to be able to more effectively project their perspective directly into us much like the static discharge. We see this occurring most frequently with children attempting to get our attention. They *instinctively* know that touch penetrates our defenses.

There is another example that many of us have seen but haven't recognized what is actually happening as it occurs. This is placing our hand on the back of someone's neck. It corresponds to dominating the person touched. Most people do this *unconsciously* but some know exactly what they're doing. Touching like this not only vents tension but conveys commands. We have seen this while an executive is walking with a younger trainee and puts his hand on the back of the trainee's neck. He is exercising dominance over the trainee. We've also seen this in an interaction between and man and a woman when he is trying to influence her for sex by pushing his projected desire into her *will* center. This is also another ploy for dominance.

The previous examples are attempts at dominance and have a connotation of negativity. But this can also be positive when two lovers are attempting to share their feelings and be open to each other. Touching the backs of each other's neck only increases the connection, their buildup of sexual tension and their energetic release.

In this case, and since it's consensual, it's not a ploy for dominance but an attempt to be open to each other more fully leading to a more intense exchange.

AFFIRMATIONS & THE THROAT CENTER

Simply because the *throat center* focuses on *manifestation* does not mean that *affirmations* are an effective addition. They're not. They exist in completely different ballparks. *Affirmations* are essentially motivated from a conscious, or even unconscious, *lack* of something. That could be *self-worth*, confidence, popularity, effectiveness, performance, attractiveness, sociability or any other number of assets or qualities that we do not perceive as being part of who we are or what we want. It is undoubtedly a tangible and time-constrained fantasy connected to the *solar plexus center*. There is a separation between what we *feel* about ourselves and what we want to *feel*. This in itself *polarizes* our consciousness. Why? Because if we *feel* incompetent and *tell* ourselves that we aren't, by virtue of the conflict we draw attention and energy to the separation and it returns the centering of our consciousness back to the *solar plexus center*. This retards our spiritual growth. Verbalized *affirmations* that don't have the backing of our belief in them through our *feeling* are doomed to conflict. It undermines the unity which is required for the *throat center* to perform in accordance with its own level of dynamics. *Without our feeling being aligned with the affirmation it can't come to pass.*

The *throat center* operates on a completely different plane. Its *manifestation* is the result of a completely unified projection. There is no lack that needs to be filled. There is unity and harmony in the finished projection. Still, many of us confuse *manifesting* with *affirming* since an *affirmation* is essentially a wish geared toward accomplishing or accumulating something that we perceive as missing in our lives. When our belief in ourselves is aligned with our projections, our *throat center* manifests power and creativity. When it's not, it falls flat, and we fall back in our spiritual development.

By the time we have grown into the *throat center*, we should be well past living in the dichotomies that are born and live within the *solar plexus center*. If we listen to the mainstream "gurus" who tell us that we must "set our intention," we will be drawn back into losing our spiritual autonomy that was so hard won as we moved through and past the *heart center*. At this point, we should know better. Setting an *intention* only creates cognitive dissonance. We either do it or we don't.

THE DYNAMIC DUO

This is the first center where letting go of security preferences, aka *unconditionalness*, becomes a tool for the spirit. In the *heart center* we have hopefully learned that a *polarized* existence cannot give rise to a "transparent" or balanced spirit. For the *throat center,* yielding toward becoming *unconditional* creates a level playing field between matter and spirit. That is, if we have no preferences in play that are designed to prevent the exposure of a low *self-worth,* the work of the combined *heart center* and *throat center* can set choices in place that will foster our further path up the *kundalini* toward our spiritual awareness and the unification of its expression in the tangible world. This obviously requires a detailed description for us to understand the relationship between the *throat center* and the *heart center.* Let's begin.

The first thing we need to understand is that the *heart center* is the mediator between the tangible world and the energy world. That is, the bottom three centers comprised of the *root center, sacral center* and *solar plexus center* operate on the principle of *polarized* tangibility. The upper three centers, comprised of the *throat center, third eye center* and *crown center* operate *without* polarity or time. When our awareness becomes centered in the *heart center,* we are faced with a monumental task: to bridge the earthly disconnect between our tangible world and our spirit or energy world.

Up to this point we have spent our whole life becoming indoctrinated and acclimated to a world where separation governs everything that we do and perceive. The lineage we have "chosen" to incarnate into provides specific karmic perspectives from which we must face all our challenges and tasks. These are set up as a life format that provides the lessons that we must work through and integrate. In advancing to and accepting the *heart center* as our new point of orientation we must now consider a perspective that is totally counter-*intuitive* to our trained need for tangible validation. It is this early tangible orientation training that has provided the direction for our lessons but is now the block to comprehending our spirit. The waxing phase of our life is coming to an end and the waning phase must begin to take precedent.

When we became successful in releasing the patterns that hid our perceived low *self-worth*, at least partially, we were able to start *feeling* what is generated by others. This was the fledgling rebirth of our capacity for *empathy*. It *was* part of our arsenal of awareness when we first incarnated but slowly faded away as our investment in protecting our *self-worth* overcame it in our early *polarizing* training. Now, as our *self-worth* became less *polarized* and truer to our nature, *empathy* was allowed to flower in the cleared space.

Empathy gives a broad picture of the vibrations that inhabit the field around us. It gives us the ability to *feel* the continuity of the energies that surround us. It is this characteristic that provides a true picture to the *throat center* of what it has to work with and disarms all the lower center *polarizations*. *Empathy* provides the "raw material" that the *throat center* uses to choose the direction that our energies should take for our clearest and cleanest human expression. What too many people don't seem to understand is that the *unconditionalness* groomed by the *heart center* is not an end in itself but a resource available to the *throat center* to direct earthly energies without the human partiality that comes with the *polarized self-worth* directives of the lower centers. This allows the *throat center* the opportunity to make projections that will aid the spiritual integration of not only the person making decisions but for the welfare of all others who are connected to their decisions. Hence, the pairing of the *heart center* and the *throat center* is a partnership "made in heaven."

One more point. It is in the *heart center* where we begin to choose which environment will have dominance over our human existence. Do we let the *solar plexus center* govern us in a *polarized* perspective or do we let the *throat center* control our life participation from a timeless perspective?

BALANCING THE TANGIBLE WITH THE INTANGIBLE

Understanding is a function of comprehending the contribution that the *heart center* brings to the whole process. Remembering back to a prior discussion, you'll recall that our current state of human evolution rests on bringing humanity's awareness and actions into alignment with what the *heart center* provides. Its main "product" is learning to be *unconditional*. With a civilization that has mainly been centered and oriented from the *solar plexus center* and lower, this is a daunting and seemingly impossible task. Our overall objective is to eventually "graduate" ourselves into aligning with the principles of the *throat center*. Integrating the *heart center* into our being first is the *only* pathway that will allow us to move from being reactive (*solar plexus center*) to purely creative (*throat center*).

Once we have matured our perspective enough to be centered in the *heart center*, our next step is to assess each situation requiring our decision to determine if our actions should emanate from the *solar plexus center* or the *throat center*. That is, should our premise for acting come from *polarized* factors generated by the *solar plexus* or by reasoning determined by the *polarity* and time free dimension of the *throat center*? The *unconditionality* of the *heart center* is necessary to make sure that neither tangible decisions (*solar plexus center*) nor solely intangible decisions (*throat center*) exhibit a bias over the decisions on how we express spirit through the world. Which perspective is truly needed to maintain the proper balance of our spirit's participation? Remember, one of the *heart center's* main purposes is to negotiate between the material world (lower three chakras) and the energy world (upper three chakras) so our choices balance our expression between those two worlds. As an example, let's examine *tough love* as one of those discriminations that require the maturity of the *heart center*.

For those of us who don't have a familiarity with the concept of *tough love* or, God forbid, those of us who might not have ever heard the term, let me provide a simple example. Imagine that you're a parent with a child who has had a few "run ins" with the law and you need to make a decision on how you will handle their most recent situation. You have two choices. You can rescue them again as you always have in the past by paying a few fines and calling a few people who might help them get off the hook or you can just let the law take its course and let your child experience their consequences themselves. Most parents just take the first course and try to prevent the disciplinary action and the police record that would follow the offense. Doing this, these parents would be following the perspective of their *solar plexus center* dictating what they should do; preventing their own aggravation and social disgrace attempting to show that they are caring and compassionate parents to their peers and the world. Aka, hiding their perceived low *self-worth* that says that they're a bad parent because of their inability to teach their children to behave better. They may also rationalize that they don't want their children to encounter the results of the same mistakes that they made as children or that they are just being good parents by preventing them from feeling the pain that they did at their age. They may also claim that letting them receive the law's response would be a cruelty to the child. All these reasons are *polarized* and self-deceptive behaviors that emanate from the *solar plexus center*. From this perspective we can see that they are operating from a *polarized* bias. Then, there's the *throat center* approach.

We can let the wheels of social justice move on and let them punish your child for their misdeeds. This will set the stage for *their* opportunity to learn that specific actions bring specific consequences. This fulfills one of the most rudimentary cycles of karma that all of us need to comprehend if we are to become centered in the *throat center*. Every action produces a response of equal intensity. This is true on all the tangible planes; physical, emotional or mental. So, if we let our child receive the response as the world gives it, won't it balance out the act that brought the child's erroneous response in the first place? Maybe. It depends on the child.

The problem that most parents have with this is that if they let their child receive the appropriate response from the law, not only will they be socially assessed by the public as having no *compassion* but, more terrifyingly, their child might stop loving them because they didn't protect them. Additionally, on top of not protecting the child from negative consequences intensifying their low *self-worth*, it will also serve to confirm an *unconsciously* trained perception that they were and still are unlovable by *their own* parents.

Low *self-worth* only functions as far up the *Kundalini* path as the *solar plexus center*. Once we start to move into being centered in the *heart center* recognizing the circumstances that led toward our having low and *polarized self-worth* presents an opportunity for us to slowly ebb them away or drop them all together through the process of our working at depolarizing our responses which is such an inherent dynamic of the *heart center*. There will be times when we slip back and forth between the *unconditionalness* of the *heart center* and the possessiveness of the *solar plexus center* as there are many *polarizations* that we hold on to that we use to define our personal security. The more we are able to neutralize them, the more solid will be our base in the *heart center*. It is from the *heart center* that the *throat center* will have *polarization* free experience to make decisions that will produce the cleanest expression of our spirit.

So, as you can see, to move into being centered in the *heart center* requires us to reduce our preferences and broaden our tolerance and perspective. To move into being centered in the *throat center*, which may be a virtual impossibility for many of us, requires that we no longer have any personal investment in *polarized* preferences and that we allow for our choices to be completely dependent on what allows the universal energy and its circumstances to move freely without any restrictions through personal preference, time or polarity. The use of *polarized* choices should only be used to manifest *neutrality* between karma creating circumstances. When we feel that we *must* employ personal preferences, we're being defensive and are operating from the *solar plexus center* which aligns with low *self-worth*. Allowing *unconditionalness* diffuses low *self-worth* and allows us to reduce our defensiveness. The whole idea is to not allow *feeling* to interfere with what the *throat center* needs to do. *Feeling* should only be used as an indicator telling us where we need to reduce being personally invested.

There is one last perspective in this application which we must become aware of and extinguish. That is, where our *solar plexus center* uses *unconditionalness* as a *rationalization for* personal preference. Our *lower mind* is very clever. It knows how to twist practical reasoning toward deceiving ourselves into believing that we are doing the proper and "honorable" thing by being preferential. Let me explain.

Commercialized spirituality has repurposed *unconditionalness* as a tool for use by the *solar plexus center*. For exhibiting our spirituality in the eyes of our peers, it has become a requirement for us to *appear* to be *unconditional* in our dealings with others. Doing so allows us to hide our believed low *self-worth* by *appearing* to be spiritually minded and honorable. It is often referred to similarly as being *selfless*. If it only *appears* that we are being generous and postponing our own preferences for the welfare of others, we can claim to be *unconditional* and *selfless*, thereby building our self-image in the view of others. In doing so, *unconditionalness* has simply become a tool for again hiding our low *self-worth*. This obviously keeps us centered in the *solar plexus center* but projects an image to the public of being *heart centered*.

Our goal at this point is to be as centered in the *throat center* as we are able. To be creative means to be attuned to whatever will make our spirit and material world integrate more easily and smoothly. Creativity for the purpose of being different will only serve to *polarize* us. All of our decisions must be free of any *polarized* influence and any kind of gain must be measured in terms of how *everyone* benefits, including ourselves. Any bias of any kind indicates self-deception. This can be evidenced in doing all for others to the exclusion of the self. This is a false kind of altruism. Consciously we already know that to do all for self to the exclusion of others obviously means we're operating on the *solar plexus center* level.

In reference to worldly correspondences, the lowest level of the *throat center* color would be powder to sky blue. The *throat center* is our first conscious connection to the *Hierarchy* with its intended evolution aspiring toward the *third eye* or *Ajna center*. The *throat center* also corresponds to the Third Ray of *Active Intelligence* in Alice Bailey's *Hierarchy* of esoteric and astrological ray energies. The planets Saturn and Earth are its closest representatives. In the Kabbalah, they equate to Geburah and Chesed. The glands most closely associated are the thyroid and para thyroid.

THE THIRD EYE CENTER

The Matrix

Modes of Operation: *Receptive, Intuitively Based & internally & externally cognizant*

The *third eye center*, or *Ajna* in *Sanskrit,* lies within the skull at the approximate location of the pituitary gland. To gauge where that is we can take an imaginary line from the place midway between the eyes and just above the brow (where women in India indicate the spot with a red or black dot) to a point directly down from the top of the head. I hesitate to use the word crown as many people assume this is the spot on the upper back of the skull where the hair grows in a spiral and men tend to first grow bald. The *Ajna center* is the place where those of us participating in spiritual practice have focused our attention in order to develop a capacity for clairvoyance (clear seeing).

If we refer back to the chart in the Landscape section, we will see that the *third eye center* is the receptive arm of the *intuitive* field. Simply put, this center is our *intuitive* "listening post" where we receive spontaneous flashes that give us the opportunity to "see" and perhaps comprehend how the universe is constructed and organized.

The *intuitive* field available to us through the *third eye center* is far more subtle than our *instinct* in the *sacral center* or our *feeling* in the *heart center.* It is non-linear. That is, it is formatted in a way that utilizes no past or future. Hence, it doesn't align with the concepts of time. All is happening at the same time or in the present. For many of us who are still centered in the *solar plexus center* or lower, this will be almost impossible to comprehend. This is because the centers below the *heart center* operate in an action-reaction mode. They require the dimensions of *polarity* and time to operate. When we get to the *throat center*, this is the first place where we have access to a mode of operation that is completely devoid of time, linearity or *polarity*. There, all happens in the eternal present. This is how the projection of the *throat center* is so different from the projection of the *root center* and the *solar plexus center*. Beyond that, the *heart center* does neither. It is essentially a listening post and negotiator between the upper and lower three centers. We use it to become aware of when we are operating through tangible or intangible dynamics.

Intuition, as the *third eye center* utilizes it, is a horse of a completely different color than how we perceive reality in our everyday lives. We touched on this just a bit under the *Landscape* section. Since it is free of time, linearity and *polarity*, it is more akin to our dreams than anything else. To understand the experience of perceiving through *intuition,* we simply have to think back to when we attempted to assess and define the actions and meanings in our dreams.

When we first awaken the dream seems clear since we are still partially asleep. Then, as we further awaken our *lower mind* kicks in and we begin to work at sequencing the events of our experience. At first, we can grab a few recognizable sequences but as we try to fit them into the linear timing of waking consciousness, they begin to blur into each other and slowly fade away. The more we strain our cognitive *lower mind,* the faster they slip away until we lose the underlying thread altogether.

Most dreams of any significance work on the wavelength of the *third eye center.* The *lower mind* identifies and comprehends our waking world through comparison. Because the *third eye center* is devoid of any separative qualities, the *lower mind* is unable to process what we've experienced in a dream. To better understand how to process our dreams we need to examine the wavelengths of consciousness: *gamma, beta, alpha, theta* and *delta.*

BRAIN WAVES

Band	Frequency	Influence
Gamma	35Hz +	Concentration
Beta	12-35Hz	Active, External Attention
Alpha	8-12Hz	Relaxed, Passive Attention
Theta	4-8Hz	Very Relaxed, Inward Attention
Delta	0.5-4Hz	Sleep

Consciousness is not always consistent. Sometimes, we are wide awake and. sometimes we are groggy or sleepy. Sometimes we're wired for speed and sometimes we are just simply relaxed and disconnected. In each of those states electromagnetic waves are generated, work at different frequencies and have an influence over us in different ways. Science has measured those waves and has found that different kinds of activities are related to different wave frequencies. The fastest has been named *gamma* and the slowest has been named *delta.* The chart shows the progression of how they are divided.

Gamma waves are the fastest starting at about 35Hz and can increase to much higher. They occur while we are concentrating. They also contribute to our working memory and provide us with selective attention. This allows us to perceptually group memories and past experiences creating correlations between events and combining similar cognitive events.

Beta waves are the "busy" vibes. They run from 12Hz to 35Hz. They are active, focused and almost exclusively focus externally. They occur when we are in conversation with others, debating and help us deal with things that are unexpected. They also are dominant in physical movement.

Alpha waves emanate from the thalamus which is very close to the pituitary gland. Their frequence is from 8-12Hz. They are very relaxed and passive in attention and lend themselves well to meditation and reflection. They tend to desensitize pain and discomfort and are extinguished through thinking and calculating.

Theta waves are deeply relaxing and bring the attention inward. They are active in REM (rapid eye movement) and dreaming. They will defocus us and manifest during repetitive tasks like distance driving or exercising. They are present during daydreaming and are mentally disengaging.

Delta waves occur during deep sleep and unconsciousness. They are usually dreamless.

My point in bringing up brainwaves is to bring attention to *alpha* waves and show where they fit in the scheme of things. So, not only do they bridge the two states but, like the *heart center*, they are receptive, listening and negotiate our awareness between our waking state (tangible) and our dream state (intangible). Additionally, an important aspect of their nature is to understand that it is vital that we use the *third eye center* effectively as it is our tendency to extinguish this state through thinking and calculating. Remember, calculating and thinking logically is a function of the *lower mind* and the *solar plexus center*. Both are *inoperative* on the *third eye center* level.

INTUITIVE PROCESSING & DREAM INTERPRETATION

With everything that has been discussed so far, we can see that an ordinary *lower mind* analysis of our dreams and *intuitive* flashes will be insufficient for us to grasp either the depth or dimension of what we are receiving in the *third eye center*. Relative to the frequency that best functions in our *third eye center*, we can see that *alpha* waves will best fit the bill. The main quality that lends itself to effective discrimination is our ability to simply be passive in our attention while observing and allowing the experience to just wash over us and play out *before* we involve any thinking or analysis. In doing this it is also best to let the experience repeat itself a number of times within us until we get the full "flavor" of what it might impart to us. For the Western mind this is extremely difficult to *allow* to happen.

In the west we are repeatedly trained to think and *be in control* of all that we experience. It is essentially foreign for us to just "let it happen." Everything must be dissected, categorized and assessed as to *why* any experience occurs in our lives and then be pigeonholed in a practical and recognizable application. *Why* implies question and solution; a dimension that only works within the format of before and after. This is antithetical to the functioning of the *third eye center*. Dreams and *intuitive* flashes are almost totally elusive to our waking mind because they don't follow the logical progression of the separation that our *lower mind* needs to establish the identity of things.

If we have had *some* success with working in the format of the *heart center*, we have had *some* experience in letting go of our need for control. Our first bout in dealing with this type of approach probably came from an experience that lends itself to "letting nature take its course." It may also have taken the form of applying *tough love* to an emotionally vested situation or simply watching animals interact where we're free of *feeling* that we must intervene because there we have no accountability that relates to our *self-worth*. We may have variations of these circumstances, however, having *some* experience in letting go propels us in the right direction.

DECYPHERING A DREAM OR INTUITIVE FLASH

When we first awaken and realize that we *recognize* that we are having a dream, it's important for us to "keep the distance" from it that we have just found ourselves in. To remain mentally and emotionally detached is the *most* important aspect of being able to assess what we have received or participated in. Remember, dreams arrive in the *intuitive* mode of perceiving. It is very different from our daily *lower mind* focus.

The word *intuition* originates from the mid-15th century Latin. Its past participle stem *intueri* means to "look at, consider" from *in-* "at, on" + *-tueri* "to look at, watch over." It assumes a measure of detachment. If we can put and keep ourselves in the position of observer, we can maintain that detachment and allow ourselves to be immersed in the *matrix* or *Gestalt* of what is occurring. It is a unified experience that is extremely fragile and adversely affected by any separative or discriminating influences.

HANDLING THE EXPERIENCE

So, when we first realize a dream or vision is occurring, *don't move!* The moment we move or change our posture, the frequency changes. Don't roll over, don't change your seat, don't move. Just stop, close your eyes again and listen. Physical movement puts us back into *beta*. When we go back into *beta* we lose the *alpha* frequency and we also lose the setting that the dream or vision was occurring in. Maintain stillness.

Next, open back up to the experience. Let yourself slip back into sleep if you can. Smiling will help you do this. Smiling is a release of tension. Hopefully you can allow the experience to continue.

If you can get this far, let the experience wash over you. Immersion will bring all the dimensions to full force. This may sound silly but ask the experience to repeat itself. Dreams and visions are entities in themselves. They have a life of their own. Remember, you are letting something into your space. In the *third eye center intuition* is something you are *letting in not generating*. It's almost like you've had a conversation with someone and you're at the point where you are waiting for their response.

If you are fortunate enough to have it replay, continue being totally in the impartial observer mode. We know that when we experience something many times, we become aware of subtleties we might not have seen when it first played. *Don't* ask questions. That will allow the *lower mind* to sneak in and will destroy the fabric of the experience. Continue as long as you are able to keep the *lower mind* silenced. Eventually the experience will fade and waking consciousness will take over. If you *feel* that the experience is important, write it down before some of the details vanish.

AIDS FOR DECYPHERING DREAMS & VISIONS

There are a few things that we can do ahead of the experience to make the process easier. First, before you go to sleep each night, replay the day's experiences *backward*. This is not something that we are used to doing. Most of our thoughts invariably focus on what is coming, what's next. But then you say, but I do think of things that have occurred in the past. Yes, you do. But you don't think of the lead up to them. Memories are segments of time. They usually offer no follow-through to what comes before or after. Thinking *backward* through our day's experiences trains our *consciousness* in both directions. It counters our habit of thinking only forward. This will allow our *consciousness* to go in any direction in our dream or vision. Collaterally, this also decreases the *lower mind's* insistent push toward keeping control.

Second, any meditation or contemplation will train us to disconnect from our chattering *lower mind*. To be able to glean meaning, subtlety and depth from our dream or vision, we *must* learn and employ detachment. That means disconnecting from our chattering *lower mind* and our unpredictable *feelings*. When either of these forces have dominance in our ability to observe without attachment, our *self-worth* becomes the palette used in our interpretation.

The state of "calm water" is encouraged by disciplines similar to Zen and Buddhism in order to reach a state of "enlightenment" which, simply put, is coming to a place of acceptance and understanding of how "things are," letting material day to day concerns freely "flow by" and comprehending our place in the world.

When it comes to an assessment of our experience, it will likely be tailored by our spirit to the cues that an opened *conscious* mind might use. Though we may use the *lower mind* to hash out the particulars, the cues will usually be sent by our *higher abstract mind* keeping us aligned with the more subtle aspects of the experience so we might be enticed in the direction of personal growth. However, the meanings will be found in a more earthly place. May I suggest obtaining an array of books that give meaning to dream images. In doing so I have found that one or two books may better align than others with images and experiences that are more in sync with how I think and how I characterize people and events. There are no hard and fast meanings for the symbols that the mind uses. Dream symbols are keyed to our *personal experience* and perspectives and will be idiosyncratic to us. When we find a book that works for us, we will likely be in sync with the author for most of the other symbols as well.

Lastly, it will be important to keep a journal. Keeping one tells our subconscious mind that we are interested in processing our dreams and visions in this way and will keep cuing us when an important experience occurs. Invariably, when we are not consistent in following through on the notice that we have requested of the subconscious mind, it drops the command in favor of things that we might be more attentive to. Looking back in the journal makes us aware of applied symbols set in past experiences as compared with current ones so we can become aware of consistent patterns and issues. We also can draw analogies to other experiences.

THE MIRACLE OF BREATH & ENERGY WORK

Let's now talk about breathing. This activity can not only aid in deciphering dreams and visions but also offers tremendous benefits to the body above and beyond its sustenance. Breathing is obviously necessary. We can live without it for only a few minutes. However, the *manner* in which we breathe can have profound effects on how we function. Let's first look at some basics.

To begin with we should all breathe in through the nose. This charges and partially cleans the air as it enters our body. The breath out is optional, through the nose, the mouth or any combination of the two.

Next, a full breath is best. That is, first expand the belly and then the chest. The breath should be full and complete to capacity with no strain. Most of us breathe shallowly and only with the chest and shoulders. In doing this we take in insufficient oxygen. When we are stressed, we also inhale through the mouth. These tendencies starve all parts of our body limiting our performance and endurance.

In breathing shallowly, we also activate the *sympathetic* nervous system which is responsible for heightening our defense system and our fight or flight response. This also taxes our adrenal glands. Our *parasympathetic* nervous system which aids in calming our nerves is enabled by breathing deeply which includes expanding the belly. The belly is where the *sacral center* is found and is responsible for putting and keeping us in balance with our physical environment. The *sacral center* is also our *Tan Tien* center which is the gathering and storage point for our *chi* or life energy. Our breathing is dynamically connected to our *chi*. When we breathe deeply into our belly, we channel and build a reservoir of our *chi* energy there. The calmer we are, the more our body becomes centered there. The *Tan Tien* distributes *chi* energy throughout the body as needed.

There are many types of breathing exercises that emphasize different parts of our energy field. The *Yogis* in India call these exercises *pranayama* and they are a dominant part of *yogic* practice. The word *yoga* means unity. In pairing the *sacral center* and the *third eye center* we can accomplish the unity between the physical world and the energy world.

Practices that may be used are for a variety of different effects are bellow breath, alternate breath, buddha breath, T'ai chi breath, breath retention, bandha locks (squeezing the throat, diaphragm and perineum), and a variety of different combinations of breathing, locks and visualizations. The Chinese also traditions use visualizations call *Small Circulation* and *Grand Circulation* to circulate and build *chi* for health and the martial arts which augments the functioning of energetic and *intuitive* awareness for combat. Ancient scriptures are rife with different methods to develop energy, awareness and focus.

At this point I'd like to draw your attention to the mirroring effect of the three lower and three upper centers. The three lower centers regulate us in the physical world and the three upper centers regulate us in the energy world. The *root center* (active) and *the throat center* (active) operate in tandem. The *sacral center* (receptive) and the *third eye center* (receptive) operate in tandem, and the *solar plexus center* (active) and the *crown center* (active) also operate in tandem. When we focus on using our *third eye center* for accessing our *intuition*, we also use our *sacral center* to prepare the body, so it is calm and ready to listen. So, essentially, our breathing is directly connected to our ability to perceive our *intuition*. As we calm the body with our breathing, we can more use the upper centers without worldly or bodily distractions. This disarms our tendency to polarize with the *lower mind*. This is also why we discipline our breath which is so essential for producing a meditative state so we may access our awareness of the energy world. That awareness comes to us through our *intuition*.

When dealing with breathing or energy exercises please do your own research and where possible consult a profession for prudent advice. One word of caution. Be thorough in your consulting and research. Misuse of these disciplines, especially in conjunction with raising the *kundalini*, can have disastrous and irreversible results on the body and psyche if used improperly.

PERCEPTION OF CONSEQUENCES

The *third eye center* also reflects a quality of "undoing." On first perusal we could assume that this might be our ability to do harm to ourselves. But on closer examination we may come to see that having a panoramic view of our perceived reality gives us an unprecedented ability to "see" the consequences of our actions before they occur. This is not to say that we have the ability for precognition as much as a type of awareness enabling us to comprehend the outcome of actions as a function of our ability to understand and envision the natural flow of energies in the dynamic interplay of life circumstances. In perceiving this way, we are able to recognize what appear to be the beginnings and endings of chosen actions with equal alacrity as a complete and balanced matrix, free of the time constraints that normally bind individuals operating on the lower levels. We, essentially, see events as having no beginning and no end but simply an inter-relative balance of forces all occurring at the same time.

Those of us who are still operating within the perceptual limits of the lower centers are generally not able to conceive of, let alone utilize, operating from an *intuitive* perspective rather than the *feeling* or *instinct* unless we have regressed from a higher level due to ego issues that have yet again to be worked through totally. Those of us who have not yet arrived at the upper operative levels only see reality through a reflection of our desires with no allowance for the unexpected outcomes or natural flows of energy inherent in our learning process. We who have arrived but regressed will have a vague remembrance that something "feels" different from what we perceive but be unable to "put our finger on it."

There is one more point to ponder. The *heart center* is the balance point between the upper centers and the lower centers. It is the point where we "crossover" from being directed by the tangible world to being directed by the inner or intangible world. Essentially, we can say that this is the point where our awareness crosses over from an external *locus of control* to more of an internal *locus of control*; from rational to irrational; from material to energetic. This is not to say that the lower centers are voided as the upper centers "take over." It just indicates that the overall directivity has shifted its point of reference from what we've accepted as our reality. When the bible says we can either worship God or mammon, it is essentially asking if we are motivated by the energetic world or the material world. Both the upper centers and the lower centers participate equally but only one or the other must "direct." The consequences of either are easily definable.

DEALING WITH KARMA & CUTTING OUR LOSSES

In health, there is a point where we are no longer willing or able to reverse the damage we might have done through poor life sustenance or harmful activity choices. In the interest of conserving energy or being able to continue our lessons under renewed circumstance, it is sometimes wiser to regroup our energies by discorporating and starting again. This mortality factor is enmeshed with *third eye center* energy in that the ability to envision the entire matrix of life encourages much more trust and comfort concerning our future passing and the fact that we will still have other lives and opportunities to gain needed awareness. We must follow the path of least resistance to allow ourselves to flow with the natural death and rebirth cycle rather than desperately resisting it which is usually the case when we are centered in the lower centers.

The idea of reincarnation may be objectionable to some, but please remember, we are examining the perspectives gained through the spiritual beliefs over the centuries by a multitude of cultures that have developed disciplines for ascending through the *chakras*. These understandings and beliefs often "come with the territory." Whatever beliefs we may hold about where we go when we pass, all scriptures talk about a resurrection in one form or another. It doesn't necessarily have to include a prophet or a deity even though most do.

"KNOWING"

Perhaps the most characteristic quality presented by the *third eye center* is the state of *"knowing."* For most people, this is probably the most irrational and puzzling occurrence to speak of. Regardless of our level of development, *everyone* experiences this at one time or another. Those of us who have trained ourselves are usually aware when it happens. Those who haven't are often not but puzzled when they do feel it.

The simplest example of this is when the telephone rings we might get a sudden impression of a person. This impression can come as a picture, a feeling, a sound, a taste, a scent or even a memory. Which comes first depends on what *intuitive* senses are the least blocked by tangible world rationalizations. This can also come as a "knowing" that when we come to a notoriously crowded place a relaxed feeling tells us that a parking space will be there for us or a table will be available at a restaurant. We might even see them in our head.

"Knowing" also comes in many other ways. When we have a strong connection with a family member, a spouse or even a good friend we "know" that they might be in trouble or need our help. For those of us that don't have this part of us as well tuned, it may just come as a shock only to find later that something difficult has happened to someone we care about.

Our *intuition* is comparable to a matrix or a spider web. It's connected on all "sides." When something occurs in it, it seems to vibrate and we "feel" it at a "distance." Remember too that in the three centers above the *heart center* there is no separation, *polarization* or time. Because of that fact everything is happening *at the same time* and our *lower mind* cannot conceive of this. Yet, in this light we can then understand how future events can be "seen." We can also understand how *psychometry* (past knowledge) and knowledge of "future" events can be some of the benefits gained in training ourselves to be attuned to our *intuition* and our *third eye center*.

In reference to worldly correspondences, the lowest level of the *third eye center* color would be indigo blue. The *third eye center* is our conscious awareness of the *Hierarchy* with our ability to perceive the universal plan and its intended evolution aspiring toward the *crown center*. The *third eye center* also corresponds to the Fifth Ray of *Concrete Science* in Alice Bailey's *Hierarchy* of esoteric and astrological ray energies. The planet Venus is its closest representative. In the Kabbalah, it equates to *The Abyss*. The gland most closely associated is the pituitary.

THE CROWN CENTER

Surrender

Modes of Operation: *Omniscient, Multi-dimensional &*
internally & externally cognizant

The *crown center,* or *Sahasrara* in Sanskrit, lies
approximately two inches above the skull in a direct
line above the *pineal* gland. Note that it is *outside* of the
body. This infers that this center is essentially beyond
the scope of human comprehension. If we look at the
pictures of ancient wisdom figures such as Jesus,
Buddha, Krishna, Mohammad, we will see what has
commonly been called a halo. The implication is that
these individuals operated on a level much more
subtle than any of the other centers and that their
physical existence was of little importance except as a
vehicle for the expression of their perception of
universal energy. As individuals, we may, at short
intervals, "glimpse" the consciousness and awareness
existing at this level but I believe that no one in the
world, save for a few enlightened souls, operates from
or even comes near to perceiving this perspective. Yet,
I will say that this is a primary entry and exit point for
energy as is the *perineum* relative to the *root center.*
These two points can be loosely compared to the
extremes of *yin* and *yang* respectively where the type
of manifestation is almost purely material or energetic.
The *yin* and *yang* interplay with its infinitely possible
combinations of energy acts through all the centers of
the body in varying degrees and combinations. We as
humans encompass all the grey areas between *yin* and
yang. In this we can see the diversity in the creation of
the universe and its ever-changing expression.

It would be pointless to attempt to describe types of perception or uses of energy in that the *crown center* includes them all in an unfathomable fashion except perhaps through the awareness of those aforementioned enlightened souls. And, even then, who would they be able to explain it to that would have any comprehension or comparable experience to relate with? Hence, I would not dare to insult anyone's intelligence by attributing any qualities or abilities to this center.

In reference to worldly correspondences, the lowest level of the *crown center* color would be violet. The *crown center* is the place where the presence of the *Hierarchy* dwells passing the universal flow of energy that we must all ultimately surrender to. The *crown center* also corresponds to the First Ray of *Will and Power* in Alice Bailey's *Hierarchy* of esoteric and astrological ray energies. The planets Vulcan and Pluto are its closest representatives. In the Kabbalah, it equates to *Binah and Chokmah*. The gland most closely associated is the *pineal* which is known to be responsive to light.

Part 4

EXERCISES FOR HEIGHTENING SUBTLE AWARENESS

To the average person it may seem like the majority of the *chakra* section is encouraging us to become less tangible. But our encouragement is not so much about becoming less tangible as it is to become less *polarized* in our approach to handling our life issues. This will in turn will allow the universal energy to express through us more fluidly and with less of the resistance that is inherent in the *lower mind's* perception of reality. Whatever reservations we have in handling our life issues invariably become the *polarizing* influences that block or prevent the neutrality needed for advancing in our development of subtle awareness.

There are things that we can do with our body that will lessen its internal stress which is responsible for inhibiting the natural flow of energy. Once our physical resistance is lessened or even eliminated, then we can work on the emotional currents and then our *lower mind* patterns that ultimately create the physical consequences of our *polarizing*. These I call intangible enablers that ultimately lead to physical malfunction (illness). Remember, all disease begins with wrong thinking and beliefs, then emotional reactions and intensification of our "off" attitudes and then the ultimate warning of misdirected energy, physical malfunction and disease. These "events" occur sequentially. When we don't pay attention to the mental warning signs, it becomes emotional. When we don't pay attention to the emotional warning signs, it becomes physical. The universe is constructed so that our misdirected energy becomes progressively denser and more apparent until we address it. The last stop is discorporation (leave the body). The simplest and most directly effective process for altering how our body operates is our breath. Let's take a look at a couple of ways to use it.

ALTERNATE BREATH

Our body does not breathe in through both nostrils at the same time. Our left side and right side naturally alternate every two hours. This is generally in sync with how the energy meridians of the body switch over every two hours also. This is a function of the yin-yang relationship (receptive functioning alternating with active functioning). Hence, there are twelve meridians that channel their energy sequentially changing every two hours during a twenty-four-hour period. It's only logical that the breath should work in sync with them. The *alternate breath* exercise balances the two halves or yin-yang components of the body more quickly than their natural changing every two hours.

Sit in a comfortable position. Make certain that your back is straight and that there are no stress points in your body. Begin by putting your right thumb on the right nostril blocking its intake and inhale slowly and evenly through your left nostril. Inhale to capacity by expanding the belly then the chest but not to the point of strain. As you reach the top of your inhalation, remove the thumb from your right nostril and block the left one with your ring finger and pinky and slowly and evenly begin your exhale through your left nostril first from your chest then your belly. Exhale to empty without strain. At the end of your exhale begin to inhale through the right nostril again expanding the belly first and then the chest to capacity without strain. As you reach the top of your inhalation, remove the ring finger and pinky from the left nostril and replace the thumb on your right nostril. Now, slowly and evenly exhale through your left nostril. When your lungs are empty, repeat the cycle with an inhale and your thumb still on the right nostril.

Alternate breath accelerates the balancing of the bodily energies. It equalizes both sides of the body and aura and creates a feeling of peace and tranquility while feeling solidly grounded. This also heightens our awareness. Things will seem brighter and clearer. This is also an excellent calmative during emotional distress.

BELLOWS BREATH

If you have ever seen a blacksmith's fire, you've seen a device that pumps air into the fire to create heat and a purging influence. *Bellows breath,* in Sanskrit called *bhastrika,* accomplishes the same task. It purges stress, stale air from the lungs making room for clean air.

Sit quietly with crossed legs and straight back. Put your hands on your knees and lock your elbows. Rest your tongue on the soft palette of your mouth *not* on the ridge behind your teeth. Squeeze the *perineum* like you're attempting to prevent yourself from urinating or defecating and keep it tight. Now, sharply exhale through the nose while drawing your diaphragm up into and behind the ribs. Continue the sharp exhalations at one or two repetitions per second while allowing the belly to relax and refill with air naturally through the nose on its own after each exhalation. After ten exhalations take a deep breath in through the nose and hold it as long as comfortable with the *perineum* still squeezed. Release the *perineum* and slowly exhale through the nose. Rest and then repeat two more times.

Bellows breath increases clarity and vital energy. It strengthens the diaphragm and the lungs and clears the airwaves. It also massages the digestive organs. There are contra-indications for some individuals with varied medical conditions. Consult a competent instructor before practicing.

POWER BREATH

(Reverse Crane II)

This is an internal exercise that gathers *chi* in the *sacral center* (Tan Tien) improving performance by almost 50%. It is something that I have personally used in the gym between weight training exercises and it is *very* effective. It is found in Dr. Stephen Chang's *Complete System of Self-Healing*. You can find it in my references section. In using this exercise I have found other factors in Dr. Chang's book to use in conjunction with his description found on page 190 of his book. Here is my integration.

It is best to sit comfortably with your legs crossed and your back straight with palms down on your knees. First, exhale completely while pulling your diaphragm up inside your ribcage. Then squeeze the *perineum* and put your tongue on your soft palate. This closes the energy circuit. Now, inhale through the nose slowly and fill up the lungs only while keeping the diaphragm pulled up and the *perineum* squeezed. Hold it and wait a few seconds to let the gases exchange. Then, while still holding your breath push down with your diaphragm while extending the belly. This puts your attention on the *sacral center* located three inches below the belly button. In doing this we are forcing the *chi* we have gathered in our lungs down into the *Tan Tien center*. Hold it there as long as you are comfortably able. Then, slowly exhale the air by allowing the belly to decompress while also releasing the squeeze and the tongue.

You may find that it is difficult to retain the breath and the squeezed *perineum* for any great length of time.

With practice over time your ability to retain will slowly increase. You can sync your count for holding with your heartbeat. This will ensure that your hold time will be consistent. I have adopted doing this exercise once between each of the weight sets that I do. I find that it gives me a tremendous recharge. You may also repeat the exercise two or three times before you do any other activities that will require endurance over time. It will also calm the spirit and clear your head. Some of us may have contra-indicated conditions for doing this exercise and should be cautious. Consult your health profession if you have any doubts.

CHI KUNG

Chi Kung, also known as *Qigong,* is an ancient set of exercises designed to move energy through the meridians that distribute energy throughout the body. They are known as the *Eight Treasures* or the *Eight Brocades.*

There are twelve meridians or channels that sequentially change their activation and are recharged every two hours as does the aforementioned *alternating breath.* With prescribed movement, attention and breathing we move our energy through each of the meridians flushing, clearing and reenergizing their pathways with "clean" energy. This clears mental and emotional stress and moves the energy in a way that begins to heal most physical malfunctions. The exercises are simple and can be done by anyone at almost any age in approximately fifteen minutes per day. The set that I am most familiar with are the Eight Treasures as described in *Qigong: A Legacy in Chinese Healing* by Dr. Dean Deng and Enid Ballin.

TAI CHI CH'UAN

This is an exercise that has been referred to as a moving meditation. Its movements are slow, measured and are a precursor to martial arts defense. Its gentle movements massage the inner organs, tones the muscles, sharpens the balance, develops patience and imparts a general feeling of health and well-being. It also moves the energy through the energy meridians cleansing and toning them. It can be done by almost anyone at any age where there is attention and focus.

There are as many forms as there are clans and families in China. The form I learned is the sixty move yang form (short form) developed by William C.C. Chen in New York. One of the best books I've found explaining the dynamics of Tai Chi Ch'uan is *Yang Style Tai Chi Chuan* by Yang Jwing Ming.

These are exercises that are completely internal and require attention and focus for their effectiveness.

SMALL CIRCULATION

This is a mind focused energy movement within the body. It can be paired with the breath to intensify and synchronize the results.

Sit quietly with crossed legs and a straight back. Put your tongue on the soft palate. Put your focus at the base of your spine. While inhaling through your nose, follow your attention slowly up the back over the top of your head to the point above your lip and below your nose. Now, switch to exhaling from your mouth following the attention down the front of your torso to the *Tan Tien center* and consciously collect the chi there and then continue to the base of your spine. On the inhale you can either expand the chest and collapse the belly (Taoist breathing = energizing) or expand the belly and collapse the chest (Buddha breath = relaxing). Your exhale should collapse the type of inhale you've selected to use. This style of breathing is called *small circulation* and activates the *governor* and *inception* meridians. The inhale and exhale should be slow and even. Further variations and explanations can be found in almost any martial arts book that includes breathing disciplines as part of their protocol.

AFFIRMATIONS

Affirmations are repetitive phrases designed to create an effect for us intending to produce a desired outcome or change. Although they may be effective, it is *very important* to understand that they can be a double-edged sword.

Consider, if you will, the motivation that declares a positive change for ourselves. It almost always comes from a feeling of lack or helplessness. If we remain focused on and continue to feel the lack that has motivated the wish, our affirmation will actually energize and increase the intensity of the lack that is felt. This will ultimately make the situation worse driving us further into a feeling of helplessness. However, if we can continue to feel and immerse ourselves in the accomplishment of our wish, it will likely come to pass. *Affirmations* can work but we must also abide by a few rules that will keep them moving in a positive direction. I will list them here but you may gain a deeper understanding if you read my article posted at: https://www.johnmaerz.com/rules-4-dynamic-affirmations.

- Focus ONLY on what you want.
- Any affirmation used must allow for the possibility of success AND failure for the mind to believe in the potential for change.
- Be clear on what you want and phrase it in a proactive frame.
- Phrase your affirmations in the present tense.
- Change up the phraseology often.
- Have faith in the process.
- Your *affirmation* must be free of conditions and have a clarity of focus.
- Lastly, what you feel when you speak them accelerates the words into an active thoughtform either creating or dissolving the wish.

Please understand that *affirmations* are only an adjunct to or tool for creating the change that you want. If it is in alignment with universal principles, it is highly likely that you will be successful.

THE LIGHT EXERCISE

Alternately called the *chakra* exercise, it moves the attention and energy up the *kundalini*. This is a conscious directive but still requires a measure of letting go. The recommendation would be "don't push the river." It is more akin to *letting* the energy move in by vacating a space so it can fill it. Each level up reflects a "density" becoming more subtle at each *chakra*. In terms of lightening our tangible world load, Lao Tzu says *the Way is gained through daily loss.*

Preparation: Sit cross legged with your back straight and eyes closed. Inhale through your nose and exhale through your mouth and nose three times. In your mind's eye, step outside yourself and see a point of light in the middle of your heart. As you inhale, see that point of light grow to encompass your heart. Exhale slowly. As you inhale again, see that ball of light grow to encompass your lungs. Exhale slowly. As you inhale again, see that ball of light grow to encompass the trunk and arms of your body. Exhale slowly. As you inhale again, see that ball of light grow to encompass your entire body. Exhale slowly. As you inhale again, see yourself surrounded by a ball of white light that expands each time you inhale. Now, relax and breathe normally. Allow yourself to move back to your center.

Exercise: In your mind's eye, see an empty chamber inside you just above your *root center*. As you inhale, pull the white light energy up through the perineum and into this chamber. See this chamber begin to fill up with white light and slowly turn red. Now swirl it from right to left across your front field of vision and left to right behind you so it circles around you. As you power your filling with your breath, feel it filling and swirling, swirling and filling and throwing off the day's debris. As this chamber fills to its capacity, a little trap door opens at its top and the red light begins to flow into the *sacral center* chamber.

See this chamber begin to fill up with red light and slowly turn orange. Now swirl it from right to left across your front field of vision and left to right behind you so it circles around you. As you power your filling with your breath, feel it filling and swirling, swirling and filling throwing off the day's debris. As this chamber fills to its capacity, a little trap door opens at its top and the orange light begins to flow into the *solar plexus center* chamber.

See this chamber begin to fill up with orange light and slowly turn yellow. Now swirl it from right to left across your front field of vision and left to right behind you so it circles around you. As you power your filling with your breath, feel it filling and swirling, swirling and filling throwing off the day's debris. As this chamber fills to its capacity, a little trap door opens at its top and the yellow light begins to flow into the *heart center* chamber.

See this chamber begin to fill up with yellow light and slowly turn green. Now swirl it from right to left across your front field of vision and left to right behind you so it circles around you. As you power your filling with your breath, feel it filling and swirling, swirling and filling throwing off the day's debris. As this chamber fills to its capacity, a little trap door opens at its top and the green light begins to flow into the *throat center* chamber.

See this chamber begin to fill up with green light and slowly turn sky blue. Now swirl it from right to left across your front field of vision and left to right behind you so it circles around you. As you power your filling with your breath, feel it filling and swirling, swirling and filling throwing off the day's debris. As this chamber fills to its capacity, a little trap door opens at its top and the sky blue light begins to flow into the *third eye center* chamber.

See this chamber begin to fill up with sky blue light and slowly turn indigo blue. Now swirl it from right to left across your front field of vision and left to right behind you so it circles around you. As you power your filling with your breath, feel it filling and swirling, swirling and filling throwing off the day's debris. As this chamber fills to its capacity, a little trap door opens at its top and the indigo blue light begins to flow into the *crown center* chamber.

See this chamber begin to fill up with indigo blue light and slowly turn violet. Now swirl it from right to left across your front field of vision and left to right behind you so it circles around you. As you power your filling with your breath, feel it filling and swirling, swirling and filling throwing off the day's debris. As this chamber fills to its capacity, a little trap door opens at its top and the violet light begins to flow up above you like a fountain. As this occurs, see the violet light turn back to bright white light and you turn it *down* around you now from *left to right* encircling you as it slowly moves down past your ears, your shoulders, your chest, your abdomen, your hips, your knees, your ankle and your feet scraping and washing away everything that the other centers have thrown off.

Now again, reverse the flow *to the left from the right* across the front of your body again bringing it up between your legs and in through your *perineum*. Return to the beginning of the exercise and repeat the process.

This exercise is extremely effective in purging the unnecessary tension that our *lower mind* accumulates and attaches to each center. It is also important to note that the colors I have assigned are resonant with the *most tangible* and *lowest vibration* associated with each center. If you see other colors when you move through the exercise, let them manifest. You may be working through varied subtleties on different centers and need to let them process through powering the individual tasks that you are working with on each center. Everyone's needs and tasks are different.

Lastly, take your time while moving through the exercise. Don't start it unless you're sure you will have enough time to complete it without being disturbed. In rushing through it we tend to get sloppy and become undisciplined. This exercise may seem very light and simple but it is a very serious and effective exercise for developing your spiritual focus and balance. You may also do it any number of times. The more deliberate and thorough you are, the more grounded and clear you will become.

Part 5 –

RESONANT PERSPECTIVES

Over the years I have written many articles and books that question what it is that we do and why we do it. I believe that if we directly examine our motivations, we will receive the keys to what it is that we must address within ourselves to find the path that will free our spirit enough to produce the finest expression of what we are doing in this earthly incarnation. These articles contain the questions that I have asked myself in order to understand my path and how I must pursue it. Hopefully, there will be a few here that will address some of the questions that you have asked yourself that will address the *self-worth* motivations within you that must be answered and disarmed before you can find the clarity and courage needed for deciding what path you must take to provide you with the highest quotient of peace and the faith in yourself. It is my wish that doing so might help you in removing the mask that we have all constructed preventing ourselves and the world from seeing the fear and fragility that we all *feel* in trusting our spirit to guide us.

Article # 1 – published October 17, 2015

ARE YOU ON THE PATH?

3 Questions to Ask Yourself

As humans all of us inevitably come to a juncture in our lives where we contemplate the possibility of there being either a goal or direction that our life "needs" to take for us to feel happy, fulfilled, but most importantly, worthy. This consideration falls into two varieties: either the means justify the *ends*, or the *ends* justify the *means*. This may seem confusing at first but if we look at those of us who feel that our life is about the journey, we might say that our *means*, the way we get there, justify the *ends* or the results that we get. If we feel that our life is about a goal, then most often, our *ends*, or the results we get, will justify our *means* or the way we get there. We could also say that it is likely that the *means* would relate mostly to our values or the intangible part of things and the *ends* would likely be akin to tangible results.

Though both methods have equal merit and deserve equal consideration, the underlying common thread is a *feeling* of fate or destiny connected to an expectation that our path through life somehow has a purpose toward an "end result." For those of us who believe purpose or reason is self-determined, we might assume that we had some sort of previous intention before we came into this life. This relates to our internal *locus of control*. For those of us who believe that we were "created" by someone or something other than ourselves, we might assume that there is a role that we are required to fulfill. This would relate to more of an external *locus of control*. Either way, both perspectives imply a path or direction that must be traversed if we are to fulfill either the journey or the goal by arriving at a place of worthiness relative to our original intention.

What is The Path? Since, in this world, we have no way of "verifying" those intentions or expectations, we often find ourselves looking for milestones along the way confirming that we are truly on target resonating with and toward our original intentions. This path is generally called *Dharma* in the east, *God's Will* in the west and *The Path of Heart* in the domain of metaphysics and popular spirituality. But again, regardless of what we call it, *The Path* is still comprised of a seemingly vague and an almost elusive quality requiring deep insights and focused quiet time that can only be achieved when we are disconnected from the commotion generated by our busy physical world. We reach an awareness of "it" through meditation, prayer, communion with nature and, sometimes, even though sex. The awareness of or connection to "it" often comes at unexpected times and "rides" unbidden and uncontrollable currents which I will label as *feelings* and *intuition* (please note that *feelings* are quite *different* from *emotions* and are discussed in the section on the *solar plexus center*). Its elusiveness can be attributed to the fact that *feelings* and *intuition* are not time bound and what we tend to call timeless or eternal. The fact that our minds are temporal (time constrained) often adds to our feeling frustration in dealing with them. There are questions that we can ask ourselves that will "tune us into" this elusive frequency bringing the elements of our path to a mentally cohesive perception. When this occurs it's like "seeing" the invisible wind but only as if by virtue of it's passing through a field of wheat. Through asking focused questions we mentally gather pertinent life circumstances forming our own field of wheat revealing our being on *The Path* or off. In doing so we might sense a feeling of calm. This will tell us that we ARE on our path. If we sense a feeling of uncomfortableness, agitation or panic, this will tell us that we are NOT on our Path. Our *feelings* are the gauge we use to determine the reliability of our internal compass. Our *intuition* is the channel for the incoming information. We must allow ourselves to have faith in these intangible parts of ourselves since our mental logic and acuity cannot effectively operate in the timeless environment of *intuition. Feelings* and *intuition* were the principal venues of our "movement" *before* the forming of our minds and even before we came into this life. Let's take a look at the questions that will bring us insight as to our position on or off *The Path.*

The First Question to Ask - Do you follow your inner urges or do you defer to the convenience and preferences of others? Many of us have been raised with manners that stipulate that our guests, our elders and those considered to be "infirm" should proceed ahead of us in our activities as a matter of courtesy. This is in line with the belief that we are here on this earth to serve each other. Where this might serve to make our daily comings and goings run smoothly and give us a planned choreography for how we should interact with each other, it does not give us a clear definition of *how much* deference we should be giving each other. As a result, those of us who have an overly humble opinion of ourselves, especially those of us with a low *self-worth*, often deprive ourselves of our own needs and preferences when presented with our assumed deference to others. This has the effect of eclipsing our personal urges for expression and action that emanate from our own individual paths. Since our direction for action on *The Path* comes through our *feelings* and *intuition*, this short circuits our inner compass and we end up moving in directions that don't resonate with where we need to be. We're off *The Path*.

Excessive humility can be a function of low *self-worth* and poor *self-trust*. The more we lack *self-trust* and the more we *don't* answer our own inner urgings toward our preferences through deferring excessively to others for *their* convenience and toward their preferences, the further off *The Path* we stray. It is *extremely* important that we listen to and follow our inner urges that we may remain on course for what our life path was originally intended. Of course, we must consider a reasonable balance between our needs and the needs and preference of others. When we reach the balance point between both, a sense of calm and accomplishment will wash over us and we will know that we are where we need to be to resonate with our own *path*.

The Second Question to Ask - Who do you answer to and why? As we are raised as children we are taught that our parents and elders hold authority over us. They tell us what we can do, what we can't do, how we should behave, what we should pay attention to, how we should perceive ourselves and a whole host rules and requirements that are usually deferential to their convenience. As children, we know that this is necessary to initially preserve our safety and wellbeing. But our parents are people too. And they have their own issues and insecurities. Sometimes their own insecurities are so strong that they need to extend their authority over who we are and what we do in order to give *their* lives meaning and purpose.

As we get older, our urge for independence and the need to "test" ourselves rises up from within us and becomes an issue. But when we reach that age where leaving the nest is the next necessary step in our growth and our parents attempt to hold on to their "jurisdiction" over us, we begin to chomp at the bit and strain against the reins. Something deep within us knows when it is time to move on in our own direction under our own power. How much *self-trust* we have been allowed to develop at that point will determine the need for us to choose between whether we fold under family pressure and stay or strike out on our own by leaving. When enough *self-trust* has NOT been developed, either path will have troubling consequences. Those who fold will move through life resenting and blaming their parents for their inability to "succeed." Those who escaped the nest will simply find others in the world who resemble their parents and their authority, transfer that authority to them and then blame *them* for their inability to succeed. Those who stay will exhibit passive aggressiveness and those who move on will exhibit open resistance. All the while and in both venues the culprit for the lack of success is still our lack of *self-trust* leading to assigning failure to a scapegoat in order to avoid the exposure of our own perceived shame and self-blame for not listening to our hearts.

The key to understanding why who we answer to is such a strong indicator of whether we are following our own path or not is the fact that when we myopically give our attention to resisting or rebelling against the rules and authority laid down by others, we ignore our own urges and preferences missing the opportunity to follow a line of direction that will move us on toward answering our original intentions for coming into this life. If at the bottom line we only answer to ourselves, which is certainly an indicator of strong *self-trust*, odds are we are well on the way toward living our own path. In following our own path we have often been labeled as being the "black sheep in the family" or "following the beat of a different drummer."

The biggest encouragement toward folding under family pressure is the fear of losing the family's love, support and acceptance. The biggest encouragement toward escaping is the potential for *finding* the needed love, support and acceptance outside the family. Both fall away when we have felt the needed love, support and acceptance of the family through being allowed to trust our own judgment.

The Third Question to Ask - How does what you're doing make you feel? All of us have done things out of deference to others or because doing so would have avoided a ration of #$%& coming from someone important to us. But in acting this way and if we are honest with ourselves, we find ourselves with a sick feeling in our stomach or even a sense of panic knowing that we're either going to end up in a situation that we will seriously regret or miss an opportunity that would put us on course for what our heart has intended for us.

The point here is that our *feelings* are our barometer as to whether the "callings of our heart" are being addressed or not. If they are, there usually falls a calm over us. We sleep better. We feel relaxed and purposeful during our daily activities. We feel patience for ourselves and others and a sense that we are not missing something by what we are or aren't doing. We feel "on target." When we stray from *The Path*, this feeling of calm and "rightness" is absent and replaced with fear, panic, regret, agita, remorse, shame, sadness, and if it has been allowed to progress too far, depression.

Following our path takes courage, insight and a willingness to go and do where and what others may often find distressing to *them*. We must walk a fine balance between what our heart tells us to be and do for ourselves and what our compassion demands of us for others, who might be unable to see or find their own path without our assistance. This training should begin in childhood but with the constant and increasing pressure to deal with things of a survival nature, we are often, and sometimes violently, herded or limited into attending things that leave us unable to answer, or sometimes even consider, the song and path of our hearts. Asking these questions and many more variations of them will bring our focus back to listening to the conversation within the deepest parts of us reminding us of why we came here.

Article # 2 – published July 30, 2015

The *lower mind* is the vehicle that enables us to deal with the tangible world. As it develops, it separates parts of ourselves and our world into recognizable and describable parts contributing to our ability to comprehend the *self*. It is through this function, our assessment and our judgment that our *self-worth* is born. Of those parts, there will be some that we like and some that we will not. If we have not matured enough in dealing with our low *self-worth* issues, we will take the parts that we don't like about ourselves and apply them to other people through the defense mechanism of *projection*. These parts now become our *shadow*. By denying them, we have placed them outside of our sphere of *self*. This *polarizes* our awareness of ourselves and will obscure the clarity that we need to become spiritually whole and mature. It is imperative that we bring these parts of ourselves into conscious acceptance if we are to create the clarity needed for us to develop spiritual wholeness and maturity. The following article describes the perspectives that our *shadow* can manifest from so we may understand its origins, accept them and bring them back to light.

THE SHADOW & THE DENIZENS OF THE DEEP

Volumes have been written about the *Shadow* defining it, disparaging it, leading us toward using it, and blaming it for the difficulties we encounter in our lives. But with so many approaches and perceptions of it I think its presence has become defocused, misunderstood and misaligned while at the same time relegated to being a scapegoat for our inability to measure up to our own expectations and those of our parents in relation to what we have been taught we should want, be and accomplish. Its existence is much simpler than what we might think it to be.

In the field of psychology Carl Jung is acknowledged as its primary proponent defining it simply as the parts of ourselves that we feel are unacceptable by our own judgment and the judgment of others and then either deny them or project them onto others whom we deem as unacceptable or who may challenge our desired image of ourselves.

Rather than convoluting its meaning further with more *polarizing* dialogue, I'd like to approach the *shadow* from three basic and seemingly unrelated perspectives. The first is what we *don't* like about ourselves. The second is what we *do* like about ourselves and the third is a "casualty" of simply being born.

The first is what we *don't* like about ourselves. In this option, almost all of the low *self-worth* issues that we formed about ourselves were imposed upon us through having negative experiences with our parents and caretakers as a child. If we were not encouraged to think for ourselves or supported in any of the decisions we made, it is likely that our *self-worth* would have been diminished. We would deem these parts of ourselves that our parents diminished as undesirable since they didn't garner their love and approval. Our next step would be to disown them, submerge them and *project* them on to others thereby forming a *shadow*.

This first scenario is probably the strongest and most prominent as evidenced in our resulting behavior. The second scenario, what we *do* like about ourselves, is a little less obvious in its results but still operates well below our level of consciousness.

In this scenario we will still have a diminished sense of *self-worth* that contributes to a lack of *self-trust* and confidence. However, it will show itself in a different way. Rather than projecting what we *don't* like about ourselves on others, we will project what we *do* like about ourselves on others. We will do this because we don't trust that we have the abilities or qualities that will enable the application of our good characteristics and believe that if we try, we will likely embarrass ourselves with poor performance. Hence, we acknowledge *others* for the good qualities that *we* possess, thereby, not risking the exposure of our believed diminished *self-worth*. These denied good self-qualities essentially now produce a different kind of *shadow* but *shadow,* nevertheless. An example would be of someone complimenting another on their skills while essentially denying their own. We can also view this perspective in terms of what our culture commonly calls *fear of success*.

Both the first and second scenarios are discoverable and "curable" through creating new experiences that rebuild *self-trust* and *self-worth*. The third scenario, a "casualty" of simply being born, goes much deeper and not likely to be discovered, understood or remedied.

In Utero we are completely connected to our mother physically and through feeling (I don't want to use the word *emotionally* as it involves many other implications much too lengthy to cover here). While we are being carried by our mother and whatever our mother goes through with her body or *feelings*, we are totally receptive to and are part of. There is no separation. At this point in our development our mind and thinking has not yet been activated or developed. We are simply two beings sharing the same *feelings* in almost every way. The only difference is that our mother is mentally active and we are not. *Empathy* between us is in full swing. We feel each other's *feelings* completely. At this point there is no separation. Then, the unimaginable occurs. We are shot into the world like a cannon where we are separated from our warmth, nurturance, protection, food and comfort; truly a traumatic experience. Once we encounter and *feel* that separation from all that we were and had, we can only imagine the intensity of the urge that springs up within us to return to the oblivious comfort we just emerged from. *This urge*, though it eventually becomes overshadowed by the activating mind (no pun intended), **never leaves us**. This urge to return to this oblivion can be called *Thanatos* or what was coined by Freud as the "death instinct." Look up the mythology of *Thanatos* (death) and his twin brother *Hypnos* (sleep). You'll find some interesting correlations.

As an infant our urge to re-merge with our mother has been undeniably intense. But as we grow, we begin to make connections to others as they present a pale resonance of that most important passed symbiotic union. These pale resonances feel better than *not* having any connections at all and *slightly diminish* the intensity of the urge to re-merge which is now slowly sinking our raw and indescribable *feelings* into the unconscious and being replaced with the rationality of our rapidly developing and *polarizing lower mind*. By the time most of us have reached puberty we have become mostly unaware of our urge to re-merge. With this urge well buried, all that is left is our attraction toward the pale resonance of our connection to others resulting in the search for other supporting unions and relationships that might fulfill it. These raw submerged *feelings* have been replaced by and transmuted to our need for love, approval and acceptance. As we gain love, approval and acceptance from others, the pain of our separation becomes somewhat lessened. Our connection to others is felt by degree. Simple acceptance and inclusion by others lessens the *feeling* of separation slightly. While on the other end of the scale, an orgasm lessens the feeling of separation much more dramatically and intensely bringing us the closest to the feeling of re-merging than any other experience except for a deep meditation. The orgasm has often been called "the little death."

When we are refused those connections to others, we perceive the enforced separation as others' judgments of our *worthiness* to be loved, approved of or accepted. It is our rational or *lower mind* that interprets this separation in terms of *unworthiness*. With that self-assessment in place the mind then springs into action looking for reasons to validate the separation or the disconnect from others. The reasons we rationalize become the qualities that we decide are unacceptable about ourselves. I'm not good looking enough, I'm incompetent, I'm not smart enough, just to name a few. The mind then either denies our ownership of those qualities or, more often, *finds someone else to project them on* in order to shed them from our own self-image. These qualities again become our *shadow*.

When we look at our projected and denied *shadow* qualities, we can see how we feel unloved, disapproved of and unaccepted. But these *shadow* qualities are only our *mental interpretations* and are representative of our submerged and transmuted urge to form unions with others through replacing our urge to re-merge with our mothers simply to feel loved, nurtured and protected again in that place of oblivion where we felt no separation. Our attraction to the opposite sex represents the strongest part of that urge and is augmented by our hormonal states. Our urge for sex can simply be seen as the most effective way to re-merge.

Our *shadow* is not an aspect of ourselves to be feared or avoided. On the contrary, it is one of our best indicators of what we need to address in ourselves in order to feel whole and creative, not to mention contributing toward improving our unions and connections with others. The best part is when we are able to recognize that the *shadow* is merely the result of a transformed urge to reunite with our source. Being aware becomes a distinct advantage through pulling our refused, submerged and projected qualities back into the light of our awareness so they *can't* operate from behind the scenes and below our threshold of awareness. In addressing them, there are no more curveballs or surprises in our reactions to and with others.

Article # 3 – published November 15, 2018

How we treat others is a tell-tale factor in how spiritually mature we are. When we treat others with respect and allow them *autonomy* over their own being, we can be reasonably assured that we are operating generally from a universal energy perspective. When we are unable to do this, we submit to the indoctrinations of low *self-worth*.

Those of us who have developed low *self-worth* by being exposed to some form of abuse either become abusers ourselves or fall into allowing our own abuse by others. Whether that abuse by our parents or caretakers is intentional or just a function of their own early training is not important. What *is* important is what training they have come away with and how they apply it to others and their own children. A *disabler* is usually not cognizant that they are an abuser. They are usually only cognizant of the fact that they must obscure their own perceived lack of *self-worth*. In doing so, they become *disablers* and abusers themselves.

MOTIVATOR OR DISABLER: *WHICH ARE YOU?*

Throughout our lives we all come across people that we really like being around. When we are around them we seem to feel up, confident, encouraged and safe. For many, we never look any deeper than just how we feel. Just the fact that we feel good when we're around them is enough to keep us satisfied with our rapport with them and coming back for more. These are the people I will call the *motivators*.

Then there are also those people whom we tend to avoid like the plague. We see them coming and we literally turn and move in a direction that takes us out of their purview. All we know is that after we deal with them we feel, deflated, depleted and discouraged. They seem to have a way of making us feel tense, doubtful, limited and sometimes even paranoid or aggravated. I call these people the *disablers* because they all seem to deflate or undermine anything we feel, say or do.

As a small codicil, I will also add that some of these people have a way of making us feel that we either owe them some sort of attention, we should feel sorry for them or even that we should feel obligated to fix whatever situation they may be distressed by.

Then, there are other people who circle within and around our radar who have a minimal effect on us as they might be benign, unimportant or superfluous as we have not yet had any dealings with them of any consequence. I will call these *inconsequentials*. Since we have a minimal connection to the *inconsequentials*, I will not cover them. But we enjoy and seek out the *motivators*, and since we have the most difficulty recognizing and dealing with the *disablers*, I will cover them first.

There are many ploys that the *disablers* use, and I have given them each an applicable name, so you may separate a recognizable *modus operandi* for each of their rapports. Their motive for acting the way they do will, essentially, all be the same. This I will explain later after we have covered a few and you can begin to see a similar underlying motivation in their patterns.

The first is the **Rule Hawker**. This *disabler* gets you on two fronts: past and future. When you tell them what you've done or are going to do, they cite all the rules and protocols that you should follow or should have followed before your action takes place with the understanding that it would only then be successful and "proper." They may say this directly or quote themselves as having followed these rules themselves while also implying or outright stating that it is your responsibility or duty to do the same. The importance of the action you intended or have already taken is now reduced to the rules rather than the excitement or pleasure of the action itself. In doing this, the *rule hawker* believes they have acquired power or superiority over you. All it does for you is deflate your enthusiasm, make you feel like you've missed something and convince you that the action you took or are about to take is somehow inadequate or improper.

The next *disabler* is the **Problem Seeker**. This is a future oriented assault. This *disabler* looks at what you intend to do and tells you what could interfere or go wrong with it. What you might hear from them is, "You know what might happen if you…?" or "How are you going to handle…?" or "What will you do if…?" or "How will so and so feel about what you're going to do?" They pose so many contradicting possibilities that you begin to think that your intended action hasn't a prayer for success. You come away from a conversation with them discouraged, dis-enthused and doubting the validity of what you're intending to do. This *disabler* will often cover themselves by saying, "I'm just offering some constructive criticism" justifying their assault and preventing themselves from feeling their own guilt in knocking you down.

The next *disabler* is the **Disqualifier**. This *disabler* is happy just to poke holes in whatever you've done, what you're about to do or what you're even thinking about doing. You'll receive comments like "You can't do that because…" or "They won't let you do that…" or "You don't have enough (money, time, resources, support, courage, stamina, etc…) to pull this off." Everything you verbalize receives a circumstance or condition that is likely not to be met by you or anyone helping you.

The next *disabler* is the **Responsibility Assigner**. This can be applied to past, present or future circumstances. What you will hear from them is "You know that if you're going to do that you're going to have to take care of….?" or "Now that you've done that you'll have to answer to…?" or "Now that you've chosen to do that you know you have to…?" or "This is something you should have thought about before you…?" This type of ploy seems to be designed to make you regret whatever you've done, what you're doing or about to do. This also is a ploy, conscious or unconscious, that makes the verbalizer feel as though they have power over you or that they know better than you.

The next *disabler* is the **Expert Echo**. This can also be applied to past, present or future circumstances. This *disabler* tells you what they've read, heard or have been shown by professionals that assumes authority over whatever endeavor you're dealing with. The result is designed to make you feel inadequate to your task. You will hear things like "In college they showed me that…" or "The guy on TV was from so and so and he showed how he became successful with…" or "My doctor said that the only way to overcome that is to…" and many other statements couched with the implication that they know the best way to do whatever you're doing, have done or are going to do and that it will only work if you follow their lead and "expert" advice.

The next *disabler* is the **Justifier**. This also applies to past, present and future. This *disabler* makes you feel that you must *justify* or validate what you've done, are doing or are about to do. From them you will hear

"Why would you want to do that?" or "You did what? Why?" or "What were you thinking?" or "Are you kidding me? You did that?" Their goal is to put you on the defensive, deferential to their authority and make you feel that you must *justify* your reasoning to them. This is de-energizing, demoralizing and depleting in its effect on your enthusiasm and motivation.

The last *disabler* I will cover is the **Sacrificer**. This *disabler* makes it seem that what they recommend, or proffer, is given at their own expense and that you should feel that you must acquiesce, so that their "sacrifice" might not have been done in vain. We often see a variation of this *disabler* in a parent saying, "I'm doing this for your own good" or "It's only because I love you that I do this for you." Changing the focus toward the *disabler's sacrifice* distracts the child from perceiving any inadequacies that the adult thinks might be exposed if their "*sacrifice*" isn't acknowledged and accepted. If the receiver of the "*sacrifice*" is an adult, they will usually feel obligated to accept what is given at the risk of being seen as unkind, inconsiderate or selfish if they don't.

All these *disablers* offer a few common threads. First, and even if they're objected to, they consciously believe that what they are offering is helpful. There is usually an underlying desire for recognition or gratitude. Second, as humans we all want to have an influence over the people in the world we live in. Sometimes this influence overlaps into a need for control as a compensation for feeling ineffective or inadequate in our own daily lives. Third, if others can convince us to align with the limits that they've created for themselves, they can feel safe and validated when they're around us. The deeper side of this third thread is that if we don't align with their ideas and methods, they may think that we could expose what *they* feel inadequate about and then they'll have to deal with some sort of *shame* for being less than what they think they should be or are. It doesn't matter if the exposure is real or imaginary. The effect of the *feeling* will retain the same power over them.

All three of these threads, whether conscious or unconscious, are based on looking to others for approval or acceptance. More precisely, values that emanate from external sources are seen by them as having more validity than their own personal experience.

There can be many variations of *disabler*, especially, since their characteristics are often paired in different combinations. These seven *disablers* and the three threads they follow are not only easy to spot but very easy for us to slip into when we're feeling the least bit inadequate or lacking confidence. The idea of following an external authority over our own inner compass brings us to an interesting divide.

In living our lives, we live from one of two perspectives. Either we believe that the world controls our fate and that we are not responsible for our circumstances or that we choose our own fate and that we are accountable for our circumstances. When we see the *world* as responsible for our fate, we employ what psychology calls an exterior *locus of control*. When we believe that *we* control our fate, we employ an internal *locus of control*. As humans, we usually have a mix of the two depending on what circumstances we are the most sensitive or insecure about and how much *self-trust* or confidence we may have in ourselves at the moment.

Generally, those who have low or no self-confidence and who ascribe to an external *locus of control* believe that they must either respond to the authority of others or they will have told themselves that they are above the authority of others. Con-temporarily, this is the land of "shoulds," "supposed tos" and those who believe that they will never be able to live up to what the world expects or requires of them.

Consequently, aligning with external rules and protocols then gives the people who follow them a perceived permission to absolve themselves of any accountability if what they are told to do which might become improper or ineffective. Offering what we've learned ourselves may come from the heart but offering it brings us to a need to be responsible or subservient. Conversely, if we feel good about ourselves, we have no need to influence or change others. This brings us to the *motivators*. Their authority is, essentially, internal and based on their own experience rather than what they've been taught or told is proper. They may recognize and follow what authority may say is externally appropriate but they generally follow their own inner promptings for what they choose to do.

From *motivators* we hear things like "good job" or "now, you've got it" or "you can do it" or "I knew you had it in you" or if from a parent "I'm proud of you." *Motivators* emphasize support and the positive and encouraging side of tasks done by the people they encounter. They uplift and energize us by the things that they say. We have no call to feel ashamed, inadequate or undeserving. On the contrary, *disablers* garner just that; *shame, feelings* of inadequacy and undeservedness but most of all, they deflate the enthusiasm and willingness of their "victims" to meet the trials and challenges of daily life. Because most of the *disabler's* activities are proffered as being "constructive criticism" while even stating that they're "just being helpful" or that they "just want to make sure that you're aware," they easily slip in and sabotage the confidence of the people that they are claiming to "help."

Motivators follow their own authority. That is, their personal experience serves as the validator for what they *feel* or think is appropriate for them. Because they have learned to have trust and confidence in their own counsel and experience, they feel no need to assert or prove themselves over others or to validate themselves by seeking external approval. Because they feel comfortable in their own skin, they are able to allow themselves to give compliments and encouragement to others should they have a mind or heart to. Odds are, they are giving from the heart but not for any recognition or from any need to cloak their own perceived inadequacy through "service."

Disablers come from a place of perceived self-inadequacy or *shame* over their own experience or lack of it. Almost all of this is unconscious. If a *disabler* is able to convince you to agree with their "recommendations" or cautions, attention is distracted away from their own history and they feel less threat of exposure. They believe that this will keep them safe from outside judgment while also giving them the perception of power over you. By acting this way, they are, essentially, doing to you what they have been trained into, namely, following others to gain approval as a valued and respected (loved) individual. Another benefit for the *disabler* is that if they can convince you to follow their "advice," they feel needed and useful; something they likely didn't feel when they were growing up.

Whether you feel that you're a *motivator* or a *disabler*, please understand that we all go through both of these at some time in our lives but eventually settle into, primarily, one or the other depending on how we feel about ourselves at the time and where we've learned to draw our authority from. Generally, those who look outside themselves for validation and confidence depends on the responses of others are more likely to become *disablers*. It's important to understand that many people who swear that they trust themselves unconsciously only align themselves with what others around them espouse as the truth and what is "right" and "proper." They honestly believe that what they are deciding is by virtue of their own guidance. Those who have learned to become confident in their own perceptions and who validate themselves through their own experience gravitate more toward being *motivators*. The urgings of others have little effect on what they decide is true for them. The key to becoming more one than the other lies in our ability, or inability, to trust and validate ourselves based on our own experience rather than what we're told or taught by others. Currently, our educational system is almost totally geared toward encouraging children to look outside of themselves or to the "experts" to know what is "right" and "proper" for their clan or social group. The well-being of their own heart is never allowed to enter the picture and is nowhere to be found in new curriculums. The consequence of this is *political correctness*.

These days, following our own inner leanings as opposed to addressing ourselves solely to needs of others has become a personal characteristic that induces a label of selfishness leading to the withdrawal of support from our clan or social group. It takes courage and a strong heart to overcome the need to belong rather than to align ourselves with our own experience, *intuition* and inner urgings, especially, if following our own drummer denies our group's expectations or approval of us. This form of social blackmail has depressed and silenced many a good soul.

To be a *disabler* means that your *self-trust* has been shut down and that you are letting the world tell you who you are and who you should be. To be a *motivator* means that you have a strong heart, listen to yourself, trust yourself and that you don't need to convince anyone else that *your* way is best for *you*, thereby validating your own *self-worth*.

Article # 4 – published April 4, 2016

There comes a time when following *The Path* brings us to a crossroads forcing us to make some tough choices. Up until now our path has been one in which we can live in both worlds while feeling the benefits of both. We still have the support of our family and friends. We've also accumulated the strength and faith of our new path. But this is in *name only*. In this state our family and friends see our current choices as superficial. They think "we're just going through a phase." They still feel that we're giving them support for their personal security. We're still contributing to the family patterns and behaviors that ensure that their family positions and beliefs are unchanged and emotionally secure. The indoctrinated beliefs between us are all still intact. No one feels threatened…until we tell them that we won't play by their rules for behavior anymore.

To break our lineage programming takes a great amount of strength and persistence. It is this programming that we initially needed to put us in a perspective that will lend itself toward the lessons that we have intended to deal with in this incarnation. This is what is meant when many in the field insist that we have "chosen" our parents. It is they who provide the environment that creates the conditions that point us toward the experiences that will activate our lessons.

Much like training wheels on a bicycle, we must eventually drop this conditioning so it will not hamper our future efforts to contend with and then move beyond the circumstances that have created our earthly situations. This opens the door toward gaining the wisdom that will empower and make conscious our spirit.

On our newly chosen path we will no longer unconditionally submit to the authority of others. We have our own ideas about life and are on the precipice of living differently. We will no longer continue to hide the reality of the self-delusion of what our programmers wish us to follow. We now call the shots as we see them. Emotional blackmail for our belonging will no longer coerce our behavior.

Understand that we are still the people who they indoctrinated into supporting their tangible world perspectives.

DARK NIGHT OF THE SOUL:

Freeing Ourselves from the Emotional Blackmail of Our Family & Culture

Sometimes in our lives there comes the realization of what we've been programmed with in our beliefs of how the world works and what is expected of us. This then comes face to face with our inner need to be authentic and true to ourselves. This can occur at almost any time in our lives as we begin to become accountable for our own lives and its circumstances. But its confrontation becomes, essentially, unavoidable once we reach midlife between the ages of thirty-eight through forty-four. Probably why so many adults make light of it can only be testimony to our need for relief when it arrives so voraciously on our doorstep. This confrontation challenges our beliefs and values about our reality and can often be a very frightening and incapacitating feeling. It often leaves many of us either panicked or frustrated knowing that something must be done but that our action, if truly aligned with our inner felt needs, might completely obliterate the security we have thus far built in this world as a result of our childhood and continued training. Yet, to step into a brighter light and consciousness, this is necessary and unavoidable.

In our younger years there is usually no one else other than our parents who are our keepers and educators. Perceiving this, their presence and omniscience within our tiny world easily encourages us to view them as gods with having all our needs and answers quickly at hand. But as adults we must, at some point, come to realize that those in childbearing years have not yet reached this midlife marker either in their temporal journey here and in that they too have not yet experienced the crisis that, hopefully, eventually leads to their spiritual freedom in discovering and following their own inner path. This often is in contradiction to what is expected of them by their unsuspecting families. This separation in timing has the effect of insuring that their journey, and ours, are a wholly independent and personal one. The most important understanding that must be realized here is that each person's journey is individual and unique and cannot be shown or instructed by anyone else. It must be listened to and felt. For those of us who realize that we have allowed ourselves to be led, this is panic inducing. For those of us who have acted independently but "pushed the river" toward what we thought was the goal based on our early training, it becomes intensely frustrating. Both paths ultimately lead initially to depression and a stark withdrawal into the psychological and emotional interior of our being. For those of us who have felt the arrival of this time early on, the journey may only take a year. For those of us well ingrained and established in our instructed set of parental values, it may take many more. And then there are others who whose spirit never ascends above the threshold of consciousness and remain trapped beneath the surface through their own fear, pride, resistance and stubbornness. This journey and its goal are not guaranteed; only our opportunity to do so.

We humans, by nature, are innately social. Following our early training guarantees our inclusion and acceptance by our clan and culture and is encouraged through our conformity toward historical traditions and the sublimation of our own needs for the good of the group. Our adherence to the needs of the group is subliminally maintained through emotional blackmail with the inference that if we don't acquiesce toward a preferred behavior, the support and acceptance by the group and our inclusion in the benefits enjoyed by them will be withheld. Additionally, fear of banishment powers a collusion that encourages us to refrain from exposing each other's perceived inadequacies thereby remaining in each other's good graces and forestalling any need to grow beyond our immediate emotional boundaries. This can be seen the most clearly when we examine the psychology of our individual family structures.

There are three effects that occur when we begin to detach from childhood patterns and assert our individuality through changing our deference toward our inner urges and *intuition*. First, when we embark on a path of attempting to be authentic to our own nature, our efforts almost always conflict with the emotional security needs of our family and our clan. We are no longer comfortable maintaining the status quo with family tradition and our parents, who have initially protected us during our formative and vulnerable years, have begun to have the effect of stagnating our individual growth and consciousness. The removal of these blockages to our growth is perceived by our family as exposing hidden perceived inadequacies implanted in them through *their* early childhood training. When those in our family and clan feel our withdrawal from our blanket validation of their preferred behaviors in favor of our own growth, their reaction is often swift and dynamic. They then re-emphasize that fact that their support and acceptance of us is only retained through our acquiescing to and continuing to hide *their* insecurities and emotionally ingrained compensations. If stepping up the pressure is of no avail, the next step is their self-defensive excommunication of us and we become relegated to the status of "black sheep" in the family.

The second effect occurs in a broader frame of reference. There is a very subtle and unspoken belief in this country that our actions should be geared toward providing support and assistance to those "less fortunate" than we are prior toward taking care of our own needs or we will be labeled as being selfish or lacking compassion. This attitude is even reflected in our country mascot, the Statue of Liberty, asserting that the acceptance and provision for those "less fortunate" than us in the world and immigrating here should be taken care of. This perspective came as a result of the original settlers of this country actually needing the combined efforts of everyone simply to survive. This "good of the many" perspective very quickly became integrated with their basic religious beliefs and is now often referred to as part of the Christian ethic. Despite its religious association, this perspective has become a very quiet and subliminal programming which also lies at or just below the conscious threshold of our secular cultural waking consciousness. This perspective has morphed into the basic assumption that if we direct our efforts toward the welfare of others ahead of our own, that the hope of gaining support for our own needs would be answered by someone else doing the same thing for us. This unconscious assumption has proven to be disastrous for our ability to muster motivation toward taking care of our own issues and forming personal goals let alone for becoming accountable for our own choices. In an extreme, this has been interpreted by a good portion of the world as our having an attitude of *entitlement*. This undercurrent asserting the belief and expectation that we should be or will be taken care of by others severely undermines the accountability we need to move easily through our mid-life crises and augments the emotional effects of our perceived helplessness generated by the arrival of our *Dark Night of the Soul.*

The third of these effects comes as we actually begin to address our own needs ahead of those of others. We not only lose the inclusion and support of our family and clan but that of our nation and peer group as well. With these three effects in play, we will come to feel completely alone and unsupported in every way. But that will only serve to intensify the urgency and the necessity for us to become accountable only to ourselves and the universe by being more *willing and able* to listen to our inner urges free of the coercive and addictive effects of the seductive feeling of belonging. Our *Dark Night of the Soul* must be passed through *alone* so that we may come to trust and rely primarily on *our own* judgment and *intuition* instead of depending on any outside sources such as social mandates or religious dictates that might tend to subvert our autonomy. This will give us full authority over our own lives and choices.

Probably one of the most difficult and daunting parts of aligning ourselves with our own inner and *intuitive* urges is the overwhelming feeling of loneliness that we fall into when we lose the support and acceptance of those who were involved in our indoctrination into the traditional and religious currents of social responsiveness. Friends and associates who can no longer depend on our blanket support for their emotionally generated security needs shy away from us claiming that we're no longer the same old comrade who supported them "right or wrong." Marriages often drift apart and disintegrate as one partner grows while the other one doesn't. As our growth alienates us from our families, they claim that we're "breaking up the family" and that we have no respect or tolerance for tradition and the way things have always been done. For most of us, becoming spiritually mature is a very solitary and frightening avenue of travel.

As we lose the support of those who indoctrinated us, we slowly garner new friends and associates on the other side of the tunnel who understand the trials we're progressing through. This feels to us as a relief to our isolation, but we must be aware that there are also dangers in the practice of commiseration over the losses of our family and peer group support. We must guard against seeing those who rejected us as disloyal and subjects for disdain. This perspective will also serve to sabotage the much-needed attitude we need toward our reliance on *self-trust*. Remember, they have not yet "unplugged from the *Matrix*. We must not fall into blaming our loneliness and lack of support on those who feel threatened by our journey toward spiritual self-hood. Passing through the *Dark Night of the Soul* is our own journey and no one else can or should be held accountable for our choices.

The feelings that dawn within us with our passage through this dark corridor eventually feed us so much independence and freedom from our previous emotional enmeshments that our path obtains a speed, a purity and new light unlike that which we have ever experienced before. With it comes an understanding and *compassion* for those of us who are still in the process of passing through the *Dark Night of the Soul* and those who have yet to do so. It also brings an unavoidable sadness in us over those of whom we have lost. Yet, we harbor a hope that they too will be able to traverse the course shedding their codependence and collusions that keep them from peeling away the layers of their trained and subsequently perceived inadequacies covering the pillars of their spiritual ignorance. Perhaps this is what Jesus actually meant when he spoke of "putting away childish things."

Part 6

SPIRITUALITY, MORALITY & POLITICS

One of the best origins of our spiritual principles is heralded from the area of Tibet. It is said that the center of the *White Brotherhood* anchors its roots in this area. From here, teachers have circulated throughout the world exemplifying the behaviors that will enable us to align us with Universal Law. It is also said that the missing twelve years of the historical figure Jesus of Nazareth were spent here in the mountains of Tibet learning the "directives" that support the essence of those behaviors that will align us with the path of our spirit. One of the oldest and greatest "documents" that was produced and then "circulated" throughout the world is *The Sermon on the Mount* spoken by Jesus and consequently enshrined in Christian history.

Although Buddhism has had an equally dramatic effect on the world as the Judeo-Christian tradition, I have chosen to unfold *The Sermon on the Mount* and its principles because it rests at the root perspectives of the west and the forefathers of our country.

It is said that "you can't legislate morality." Even so, our Constitution seems to be one of the best conjunctions of Universal Law and manmade law ever produced. Our Constitution is replete with some of the best aspects of Judeo-Christian tradition espoused in *The Sermon on the Mount*.

Although the *Ten Commandments* seem to be the precursor to our national morality, *The Sermon on the Mount* offers a much more refined rendition of the human behaviors that are aligned with Universal Law. It is for this reason that I offer my interpretation of its meaning and principles.

So, what follows is a number of quotations from *The Sermon on the Mount*. They may be out of sequence from the original text since I am grouping them in relation to the attitudes and emotional patterns that were prominent during the time that Jesus of Nazareth was speaking. My explanations are assumptions on my part of what I think he was addressing in terms of Universal Law.

APPROVAL & RECOGNITION

"So, when you give to the needy, do not announce it with trumpets, as the hypocrites do in the synagogues and on the streets, to be honored by others. Truly I tell you, they have received their reward in full. But when you give to the needy, do not let your left hand know what your right hand is doing, so that your giving may be in secret. Then your Father, who sees what is done in secret, will reward you."

"And when you pray, do not be like the hypocrites, for they love to pray standing in the synagogues and on the street corners to be seen by others. Truly I tell you, they have received their reward in full. But when you pray, go into

your room, close the door and pray to your Father, who is unseen. Then your Father, who sees what is done in secret, will reward you. And when you pray, do not keep on babbling like pagans, for they think they will be heard because of their many words. Do not be like them, for your Father knows what you need before you ask him."

"When you fast, do not look somber as the hypocrites do, for they disfigure their faces to show others they are fasting. Truly I tell you, they have received their reward in full. But when you fast, put oil on your head and wash your face, so that it will not be obvious to others that you are fasting, but only to your Father, who is unseen; and your Father, who sees what is done in secret, will reward you."

The preceding quotes appear to address our need for recognition and approval. These qualities originate through having an outer or external attention aligned with a primarily external *locus of control*. People of this type of focus place more value on what others think of them than what they think about themselves and usually give away their autonomy and authority by seeking the recognition and approval of others. In seeking approval, it becomes evident that they are most likely coming from self-doubt and depending on their extreme, low *self-worth*.

The consequence of having low *self-worth* requires the support and approval of others simply in order to feel valid, adequate and worthy. Jesus is attempting to get his listeners to, first, bring them to the awareness that they are doing this and, second, terminate the perspective. Terminating this perspective short circuits the snowball effect of continuing to diminish their *self-worth*. As lowering their *self-worth* eases, the ability to trust *their own* judgment becomes more available. This will ultimately allow their inner spirit to permeate their consciousness.

THE COURAGE OF OUR CONVICTIONS

"You are the light of the world. A town built on a hill cannot be hidden. Neither do people light a lamp and put it under a bowl. Instead, they put it on its stand, and it gives light to everyone in the house. In the same way, let your light shine before others, that they may see your good deeds and glorify your Father in heaven."

Belonging is the best protection for hiding our differences. When our differences are exposed and translated into inadequacies by others, it leads them to ostracize us from the clan. Revealing our perceived lack of *self-worth* is terrifying to those of us that have the belief that we might be unlovable.

Our culture has evolved to support whatever constructed fantasies each of us may have about ourselves. As long as our differences are not exposed to others, our low *self-worth* can remain hidden. Avoiding this ensures our sense of protection and belonging. This then can be equated to our being loved and approved of.

If we make apparent or enlighten others as to the defensive emotional patterns that hide their perceived *unworthiness, we* become a threat to *them*, and they will subject us to "cancel culture." In the family, we call these people the *black sheep of the family* since they no longer play by the rules that we've set in place that hide our perceived differences. In the world outside the family, these people become outcasts. Most people play along so as not to be noticed as "being different," hence, they don't become a threat to others.

Jesus of Nazareth appears to be aware of this emotional pattern and is encouraging others to step beyond their need for belonging and risk bringing the truth to light. The *black sheep of the family* usually become the teachers of the entire clan. They potentially can bring their clan to a level of emotional maturity if they are able to persevere and resist the need to belong. Jesus appears to be aware of this dynamic and is encouraging others to also become teachers in their families. When there is no longer a need to hide our *shadow*, spiritual maturity has an open door to flourish.

POLARIZATION

"You have heard that it was said, 'Eye for eye, and tooth for tooth.' But I tell you, do not resist an evil person. If anyone slaps you on the right cheek, turn to them the other cheek also. And if anyone wants to sue you and take your shirt, hand over your coat as well. If anyone forces you to go one mile, go with them two miles. Give to the one who asks you, and do not turn away from the one who wants to borrow from you."

"Do not judge, or you too will be judged. For in the same way you judge others, you will be judged, and with the measure you use, it will be measured to you."

"Why do you look at the speck of sawdust in your brother's eye and pay no attention to the plank in your own eye? How can you say to your brother, 'Let me take the speck out of your eye,' when all the time there is a plank in your own eye? You hypocrite, first take the plank out of your own eye, and then you will see clearly to remove the speck from your brother's eye."

Polarization is the most potent anchor for living in the tangible world. It keeps us bonded to the separative influences of the *lower mind* and restricts the entrance of our unconditional spirit into our consciousness.

We've been told that in *Genesis 1:28* that our creator told us to *be fruitful multiply*. But now, in order to reunite with our spirit, we must reverse that mandate. We must change our path of *involution* toward *evolution* if we are to return to our spirit. But we must also do that individually as our movement toward spiritual growth and maturity is a personal task related only to our own incarnations. To gain awareness, we must reverse the *karmic wheel* and now neutralize all the circumstances that have led to the creation of our *polarized* consciousness'. In the *Tao Te Ching* passage number four says:

> The Way is a void,
>
> Used but never filled:
>
> An abyss it is,

Like an ancestor

From which all things come.

It blunts sharpness,

Resolves tangles;

It tempers light,

Subdues turmoil.

A deep pool it is,

Never to run dry!

Whose offspring it may be

I do not know:

It is like a preface to God.

The *polarized* influences we received in the upbringing of our lineage have given us direction toward our chosen lessons and led us to our current awareness. Now to make sense of our path, we must neutralize the *polarities* so we can comprehend the unity in which we find ourselves. This means yielding to the conflicting forces that surround us in the tangible world if we are to make our spirit manifest in our consciousness.

Jesus of Nazareth appears to understand that the separations we harbor between us are the major stumbling blocks to acquiescing to our spirit. These separations or *polarizations* keep us locked in the tangible world so we can't see the unity that Universal Law makes available to us. Our resistance to others keeps the tangible world in charge of our consciousness.

So, in worldly tangible terms, if someone hits you, turn away. If they insult you, ignore them. If they steal from you, let them have it. If they ask something of you, give it. The idea is to refrain from action that will create *polarization* or resistance. Jesus apparently understood Newton's third Law of Motion that states that *for every action there is an equal and opposite reaction* even before Newton came on the scene. And also, so did the Chinese. In the Taoist the practice of Tai Chi Chuan the same is accomplished. It is also based on the absence of resistance in order to allow the redirection of the energy of their opponent in a more beneficial purpose for the practitioner.

TRUSTING OUR SPIRIT

"Therefore I tell you, do not worry about your life, what you will eat or drink; or about your body, what you will wear. Is not life more than food, and the body more than clothes? Look at the birds of the air; they do not sow or reap or store away in barns, and yet your heavenly Father feeds them. Are you not much more valuable than they? Can any one of you by worrying add a single hour to your life?

"And why do you worry about clothes? See how the flowers of the field grow. They do not labor or spin. Yet I tell you that not even Solomon in all his splendor was dressed like one of these. If that is how God clothes the grass of the field, which is here today and tomorrow is thrown into the fire, will he not much more clothe you—you of little faith? So do not worry, saying, 'What shall we eat?' or 'What shall we drink?' or 'What shall we wear?' For the pagans run after

all these things, and your heavenly Father knows that you need them. But seek first his kingdom and his righteousness, and all these things will be given to you as well. Therefore do not worry about tomorrow, for tomorrow will worry about itself. Each day has enough trouble of its own.

In our western culture, trusting something that is not tangibly defined is a hard pill to swallow. When it comes to people, we have been taught to trust that only our parents, the authorities (our surrogate parents) or "the experts" know what actions are proper for dealing with our life issues. Also, at this point in our history, many of us have even gone so far as to accept that we are *not* to trust our own experience.

In the time that Jesus of Nazareth was speaking, not much has changed. Then, as it is now, our tendency is to trust only that reality is dependent on the *lower mind's* interpretation of what is tangible. Our resistance to and fear of being out control is a primary driver for our consciousness. Worry is a consequence of that fear. He asks us if that worry will change anything. For them and us, trusting that the universe will provide us with a practical path into the future is felt not to be an option.

When we obsess over that control, our spiritual awareness has no place to enter. We stay wound up like a clock fearing that we will not only be unable to handle life's circumstances but that others will see that and assume that we are inadequate for the task of living. Worry and low *self-worth* are primary indicators that our *lower mind* is in charge of our consciousness.

Our indoctrination into life through our family lineage is a powerful factor in ensuring that we will trust only what is tangible. It takes many years for us to come to the understanding that there is much more to life than what we can see or hold in our hands. Many of us never arrive there. Trusting that the universe, or if you choose, God, will provide the path is probably one of the hardest beliefs to accept and live by. The *lower mind* is only a tool. Yet, through our indoctrination we have given it such a place of importance that we have come to believe that we *are* our *lower minds*. Rather than accepting "mind over matter" we must come to believe that "spirit over matter" is the only path that will manifest that part of ourselves that we have come here to accomplish. To do this, we must acknowledge that there is much more to life than what our senses are telling us.

If we can stop the worry and just accept life as it comes to us and just trust that our spirit has put us in the right place for what we need to learn, we can free ourselves from the pain. As Buddha has told us, pain comes from desire and the resistance we pose toward attaining it. Letting go of the need to control is the hardest thing any of us can *will* ourselves to do. In *this* case, we have control.

ACTIONS SPEAK LOUDER THAN WORDS

"Do not give dogs what is sacred; do not throw your pearls to pigs. If you do, they may trample them under their feet and turn and tear you to pieces.

"Watch out for false prophets. They come to you in sheep's clothing, but inwardly they are ferocious wolves. By their fruit you will recognize them. Do people pick grapes from thornbushes, or figs from thistles? Likewise, every good tree bears good fruit, but a bad tree bears bad fruit. A good tree cannot bear bad fruit, and a bad tree cannot bear good fruit. Every tree that does not bear good fruit is cut down and thrown into the fire. Thus, by their fruit you will recognize them.

"Not everyone who says to me, 'Lord, Lord,' will enter the kingdom of heaven, but only the one who does the will of my Father who is in heaven. Many will say to me on that day, 'Lord, Lord, did we not prophesy in your name and in your name drive out demons and in your name perform many miracles?' Then I will tell them plainly, 'I never knew you. Away from me, you evildoers!'

Not everyone *walks their talk.* Many simply *talk their walk* expecting that you will trust that what they say, is what they will do. We should never trust that what *everyone* says is true or that they will do as they say. Talk is cheap. Their actions speak a lot more loudly than their words. This is not to say that we must not trust their words but that we must not expect their actions. In a wider focus, we can say that it's best that we allow ourselves to expect the unexpected.

Often, what is said by some people is merely a ruse to gain your trust in them. It is likely that they have been lied to themselves in their upbringing by people they have been taught to believe will honor their words. For those who taught them, and for those who have also learned to lie through their example, they have learned that this is the only way to obtain what they want. This behavior unconsciously fosters the assumption that they don't deserve what they ask for and that their only alternative is that they must deceive others in order to attain it.

We must come to the understanding that when someone lies to us, they don't trust that we will believe them or that they will be viewed by us as a person who is worthy of what they are asking for. Those of us who feel we must put blind trust in others often have little or no trust in ourselves. So, the need to lie comes from low *self-worth*.

Jesus of Nazareth is telling us to observe others and we will know them by the experience we have with them. He is telling us to trust our heart more than the words of others. If we're quiet and observant, we can almost always feel what's below the surface of what is being said.

We should always believe and choose to do what *we* think is right. Hearsay is often poison to the heart. Those of us who blindly put our faith in others are often disappointed and ultimately are the ones who have little faith in ourselves. Honesty is the best policy. If we are true to ourselves, our spirit can shine through.

GOD OR MAMMON

"Do not store up for yourselves treasures on earth, where moths and vermin destroy, and where thieves break in and steal. [20] But store up for yourselves treasures in heaven, where moths and vermin do not destroy, and where thieves do not break in and steal. [21] For where your treasure is, there your heart will be also.

"No one can serve two masters. Either you will hate the one and love the other, or you will be devoted to the one and despise the other. You cannot serve both God and money.

This is probably one of the best-known quote from *The Sermon on the Mount*. For the students and disciples on *The Path*, it is the best understood. For the denier of our spirit and the intangible world, it is the most widely ignored.

The choice that is asked for requires a dedication to accepting and supporting *Universal Law*. To do so abandons the pursuit of wealth and recognition permeating worldly influence in favor of aligning with the energetic spirit that is providing our lessons of transition through the tangible worldly environment. As the *lower mind* is to the higher and more subtle *abstract mind,* the worldly environment is to the spiritual realm. They are simply tools in a staging area ultimately leading us toward our path back to Universal Unity. The best "real world" comparison would be Socrates' *Allegory of the Cave* where their *shadows* were more revered and respected than the source of light that produced them. When we put all our faith and belief into the workings of the tangible world, it is like having faith and belief in only the *shadows* projected on the cave walls. They are only reflections of the source. Spiritual maturity only comes when we understand and accept this reality. Jesus of Nazareth is asking the people to simply accept the *will* behind their inner spirt which works in ways that are not yet comprehensible to them. He is asking them to trust that the universe will provide what they need to transition through their worldly environment by not surrendering to their *lower mind's* need to control it. He is asking them to trust in something much wider and more permeating than their own personal efforts: their spirit.

CLOSING THOUGHTS

The dynamics of spiritual maturity carry through every avenue of our earthly life. And every part of our existence overlaps every other. What we say, do, think, feel, intuit, inhale, digest, pay attention to, ignore, love, hate, assume, believe, desire and avoid are interrelated with every other dimension of how we choose to participate or not. Life is a Gestalt of influences that have virtually no boundaries. Yet, our *lower mind* believes that we can control our lives and how we are responded to by the world. How we perform in each of these dimensions either neutralizes our *polarizations* creating greater subtle awareness or exacerbates its "permanence" creating greater grossness and *decreasing* our subtle awareness.

At the root of every one of these dimensions we must choose to either follow the world and its demands on us, which will only increase our "karmic" imbalance, or support the autonomy of our spirit which will align us with Universal Law and rebalance our energies after having worked through our past beyond our lineage programming.

There are those of us who know. There are those of us who don't know. There are those of us who know we don't know and there are those of us who don't know that we don't know. We must judge for ourselves which reality fits us and work from there.

For those of us who are on *The Path* and are actively working to align with our spirit and the universal energies it draws through us, the above statements will make sense. For those of us who are unable to make sense of what I said, the four articles that I have included exemplify life scenarios that might bring us to a sensing of where we should be, why and how we should act in order to comprehend our place and our "karmic" tasks in the life we have chosen to incarnate into. In this light I offer a quote from Lao Tzu: "*The Way* is gained through daily loss." If you can understand this, you are blessed.

REFERENCES & HELPFUL READING MATERIAL

Alcyone (Jiddu Krishnamurti) (1910). *At the Feet of the Master*. Theosophical Publishing House, Wheaton, Illinois. ISBN# 978-1387971459.

Anonymous (Joseph S. Benner) (1927). *Brotherhood: An Impersonal Message*. DeVorss & Co., Marina del Rey, California. ISBN# 0-87516-300-9.

Anonymous (Joseph S. Benner) (1914). *The Impersonal Life*. DeVorss & Co., Marina del Rey, California. ISBN# 978-9351285229.

Anonymous (Joseph S. Benner) (1971). *The Way Out: The Way Beyond, Wealth & The Teacher*. C.A. Willing., San Gabriel, California. ISBN# 978-0875163024.

Beattie, Melody, (1986). *Codependent No More: How to Stop Controlling Others & Start Caring for Yourself*. Hazelden Books, Center City, Mn. ISBN# 0894-864-025.

Berne, Eric (1964). *Games People Play: The Basic Handbook of Transactional Analysis*. Ballantine Books, Random House, New York, NY. ISBN# 0-345-41003-3.

Blakney, Raymond B., (1955). *The Way of Life Lao Tzu: Tao Te Ching: A New Translation*. Mentor Books, Chicago, Illinois. LCCC# 55-7401.

Bradshaw, J. (1988). *Healing the Shame that Binds You.* Health Communication Books, Inc., Deerfield Beach, Florida. ISBN# 978-0-7573-0323-4.

Chang, Stephen T., (1986). *The Complete System of Self-Healing Internal Exercises.* Tao Publishing, San Francisco, California. ISBN# 0-942196-06-6.

Deng, Dr. Dean Y. & Ballin, Enid. (1998). *Qigong: A Legacy in Chinese Healing.* Qigong International Publications, New Orleans, La. ISBN# 0-9657560-8-4.

Forward PhD., Susan. (1989). *Toxic Parents: Overcoming Their Harmful Legacy and Reclaiming Your Life.* Random House, New York, N.Y. ISBN# 978-0-553-38140-1.

Forward PhD., Susan. (1997). *Emotional Blackmail.* Harper Collins Publishers, Inc. New York, NY. ISBN# 978-0-06-092897-1.

Harris, Thomas, (1967). *I'm OK – You're OK.* Harper Collins, New York, N.Y. ISBN# 0-06-072427-7.

Krishnamurti, Jiddu, (1969). *Freedom from the Known.* Harper Collins Publishers, New York, New York. ISBN# 978-0-06-064808-4.

Maerz, John L., (2014). *Energizing Self-Trust: 7 Steps for Reclaiming Your Power.* Emotional Troubleshooter, Sarasota, Fl. ISBN# 978-0986-436-451.

Maerz, John L., (2018). *Out of the Box: 7 Elements for Raising a Self-Directing Child.* Emotional Troubleshooter, Sarasota, Fl. ISBN# 978-0986-4380475.

Maerz, John L., (2020). *Ploys for Dominance: A Guide for Recognizing & Disarming Manipulation.* Emotional Troubleshooter, Sarasota, Florida. ISBN# 978-0986-436-437.

Miller, Alice, (2002). *For Your Own Good: Hidden Cruelty in Child-Rearing and the Roots of Violence.* Farrar, Straus & Giroux, Frankfurt, Germany. ISBN# 0-374-52269-3.

Osho (Bhagwan Shree Rajneesh). (1999) *Maturity: The Responsibility of Being Oneself.* St. Martin's Griffin, New York, New York. ISBN# 978-0312205614.

Robbins, Anthony, (1986). *Unlimited Power.* A Fireside Book Published by Simon & Schuster. New York, N.Y. ISBN# 0-684-84577-6.

Seligman, M.E.P., Maier, Steven F., Peterson, Christopher, (1993). *Learned Helplessness: A Theory for the Age of Control.* Oxford university Press. New York, N.Y. ISBN# 0-19-504467-3.

Three Initiates, (1912). *The Kybalion: A Study of the Hermetic Philosophy of Ancient Egypt and Greece.* The Yogi Publication Society, Chicago, Illinois. ISBN# 978-0943217215.

Watts, Alan, (1966). *The Book: On the Taboo Against Knowing Who You Are.* Vintage Books, Random House, Inc., New York, N.Y. ISBN# 0-679-723000-5.

Watts, Alan, (1951). *The Wisdom of Insecurity.* Pantheon Books, Random House, Inc., New York, N.Y. ISBN# 0-394-70468-1.

John Lawrence Maerz is an author, instructor, professional speaker and coach with specializations in metaphysics and psychology. His extensive background in metaphysical disciplines includes astrology,  tarot, numerology, I-Ching, energy work, martial arts, psychic development and mediumship.

John has worked as a counselor and case manager with teen substance abuse, in child protection services and is a seasoned personal coach and adviser with diverse experience in the field of human potential. He incorporates and integrates personality influences, shadow work, nutritional needs, creative expression and personal desires while uncovering his client's innate abilities and potential.

John co-owned and successfully ran Starchild, a metaphysical bookstore in Port Charlotte, Florida, for over a decade. He also co-owned and ran the Astrological Institute of Integrated Studies begun in Bayshore New York, a school teaching a multitude of metaphysical subjects from 1983-2005. He is dedicated to raising awareness and sharing his own unique perspective and understanding about life's journey and its meaning. He recognizes and emphasizes the importance of having balance and accountability. He challenges his students and clients to keep fulfilling their spiritual potential through their own individual experiences.

Over the years, John has produced a series of books, workshops, lectures and seminars presenting different metaphysical topics in print and on MP3. These materials are available on www.JohnMaerz.com. He is also a voracious writer and has written more than 70 articles on many thought-provoking subjects which are also available on his site. He has also published thirteen books on metaphysics and psychology. All books are available through Amazon.

You can contact John at (941) 286-1562

www.JohnMaerz.com

9 781737 249382